Wallace-Homestead Price Guide to

AMERICAN
Country
ANTIQUES

Wallace-Homestead Price Guide to

AMERICAN *Country* ANTIQUES

B O O K   1 4

DON & CAROL RAYCRAFT

Wallace-Homestead Book Company
Radnor, Pennsylvania

Contents

Acknowledgments

A project of this magnitude requires a great deal of cooperation. Without the assistance of the individuals listed below it could not be completed. We sincerely appreciate their help and friendship.

Teri & Joe Dziadul
Dr. Joseph MacMillan
Dr. Alex Hood
Opal Pickens
Mary Ellen Wilson
Bruce & Vicki Waasdorp
Judith Lile
Garth's Auction
Tom Porter
Jim White
American Roots
Manuela Yokota
Ellen Tatem
Lancaster Antique Market
Quail Country Antiques
Keith Wixson
Nina Wixson
Sue Lynch
Sharon Palombo
Sharon Morris
Connie Sayers
Larry Kruppenbacher
Judy Kruppenbacher
Mary Millman
Matthew Millman

Jewell Schrang
Bonnie Wixson
Copake Country Auctions
Michael Fallon
Ken & Carllene Elliott
Raymond & Nancy Gerdes
Bernie Green
Ann Roop
Brenda Humphrey
Jerry Jeff Walker
Allen Hanson
Linc Hanson
Leslie Look
Dick & Kay Thompson
Mary Heaton
Kathy Liston
Carol Donoghue
Marlene Hegeman
Ellie Van Voorhis

Introduction

In the mid-1960s we were both teaching school in a small town in the middle of Illinois and were driven, though seriously inexperienced, collectors of "primitives." Primitives were defined by every 70-year-old antiques dealer in North America in 1966 as the junk on the back porch or in the basement of the shop that was left over after the Depression glass, oak rocking chair, and collection of hatpins were removed from the recently purchased estate and added to the inventory.

Between us we made almost $11,000 a year, but that went a long way on 45¢ Whoppers at Burger King, 30¢ gasoline, and $75 pine dry sinks.

Many of the dealers with whom we came into contact in our persistent travels across the heartland of America went out of their way to share their life experiences and knowledge with us. For absolutely no additional charge we want you to possess the fundamentals we learned at the feet of myriad dealers of primitives and carnival glass.

The 45¢ Whopper has gone the way of the passenger pigeon, but these four eternal truths will remain as long as there is someone searching for the $75 pine dry sink.

We gave up long ago.

The Four Eternals

1. Provenance—Make every effort to find out where a piece was originally made and who has owned it. This is always longer than a long shot.

2. Condition—If the condition is less than pristine, look for another one. Don't buy somebody else's problems.

3. Degree of rarity—Have an appreciation for what separates the common from the uncommon. Buy the uncommon.

4. Finish—The original finish should be intact. If a piece has been dipped, scraped, skinned, or stripped, you don't want to own it. In today's marketplace the quality of the original painted finish on a piece of furniture determines its level of desirability.

CHAPTER ONE

Predictions, Speculations, and Trends

In our travels over the past two years and in conversations with dealers and collectors from across America, we have heard, digested, thought about, and reached the ten conclusions that appear below.

1. The number of "open" antiques shops will continue to decline.

An open shop is an antiques business that maintains regular hours at an advertised address. Twenty-five years ago most purchases were made at open shops, but things have changed. The rise of antiques and collectibles malls has given open-shop owners an alternative to maintaining a regularly scheduled business.

In some urban and rural environments potential insurance and security difficulties have made the mall atmosphere much more attractive to many dealers.

2. The number of "group" shops will gradually increase.

A group shop is created when three to seven or eight dealers decide to jointly rent a facility, pool their merchandise, and share time working in the business. Typically the group shop carries antiques that fit into specific categories.

It is not unusual for a group of dealers who specialize in Americana to put together a shop. The advantage of this operation is that the dealer on hand to wait on you probably has some knowledge and can answer your questions about the merchandise. In an antiques/collectibles mall this is the exception rather than the rule.

3. The number of mail and telephone auctions is going to increase.

Baseball card and memorabilia collectors and dealers have been taking part in mail and telephone auctions for a decade. The procedure typically involves making available an illustrated catalog with estimated values for each item and a minimum bid necessary to open the bidding. Both telephone and mail versions are conducted over a specific time frame and the highest bidder at the conclusion buys the item. Occasionally a buyer's premium is added to the successful final bid.

4. In the short run the number of antiques and collectibles malls will continue to grow.

To many potential entrepreneurs the concept of the antiques mall appears to be almost too good to be true. The procedure for starting this type of business is to find a large building (empty grocery store, discount store, factory, mill) with favorable rent and some traffic flow in the immediate area. Dealers are recruited to lease space and are assessed a monthly fee based on the size of their booths. The advantage of the mall is that each dealer does not have to be physically present to sell his or her merchandise. Some malls do require their dealers to work a specific number of hours each month to control labor costs, and dealers may be required to pay a percentage of their gross monthly sales to help with advertising.

For the mall to be successful it is essential that every effort be made to maintain quality-control standards. If the mall managers or operators are more concerned with the number of dealers rather than the quality of the merchandise they offer for sale, the mall will turn into a thrift shop and the doors will inevitably close.

In the long run the malls that survive by recruiting dealers with better things to sell can be mutually profitable for all involved in the operation.

5. There is a tendency for some upscale dealers to borrow the tailgate concept by renting a commercial space near the site of a prestigious urban show and offering their merchandise in a gallery setting.

The limited-run gallery approach makes a great deal of sense because serious collectors attend the show and are more than willing to walk across the street or around the corner to possibly find another piece for their collection.

6. The number of dealers who specialize in a particular segment of the

Americana market and who issue price listings or catalogs of items that they have for sale by mail is increasing and will continue to flourish.

7. The tailgate shows that operate within close proximity (often within walking distance) to heavily advertised and established shows will continue to prosper.

The classic example of a successful tailgate operation occurs in Nashville each winter with independent shows opening at the Ramada Inn and Fiddlers Inn prior to the Heart of Country show at the Opryland Hotel. Dealers fill the rooms of both motels and offer for sale a staggering variety of Americana. The three independently promoted events draw nationally because of the numbers of dealers, the quality of the merchandise, and the geographic proximity to Nashville that encourages visitors and buyers from both coasts.

8. Rather than automatically assigning a collection or a single piece of furniture to an auction house, some collectors allow a dealer to sell for them on consignment.

In a consignment sale the dealer and owner determine how much the owner "has to have" and the piece is offered in the dealer's shop or booth at an antiques show or market. When the piece is sold, the dealer pays the owner the agreed upon price.

9. The number of speciality antiques shows will continue to grow.

A speciality show brings together dealers offering a single broad category of antiques (Americana, advertising, Depression glass, art glass, art pottery). Historically, most antiques shows have been more general in orientation, offering diverse merchandise that crosses all categories.

The tendency is for the gate at the speciality show to be smaller for the promoter, but the buyers who attend are interested in making purchases and not merely browsing for entertainment.

10. As prices continue to climb and concerns about fakes and repainted country furniture abound, many collectors are now seriously looking for seminars, books, and videotapes that can enhance their knowledge and help them avoid some costly mistakes in building their antiques holdings.

Price Guides

The purpose of any price guide is to provide the reader with the approximate value of a given item. A price guide should be used much like an auction catalog that contains an estimate of an item's value. The auctioneer includes an estimate to help potential bidders gain some perspective about values and to hint about what to expect to pay on auction day.

Our price guide assumes that the item pictured or described is in at least excellent, original condition and, unless otherwise noted, the value listed reflects that condition. Prices given are approximately those for which the items were offered for sale in a shop or mall or the price the piece has actually brought at auction. Each year we contact nationally known dealers, collectors, and auction houses from diverse areas of the United States to assist us.

Ultimately, the true value of a country antique, truss, or used car is determined at the point of sale between the buyer and seller.

CHAPTER TWO

Antiques 103:
Another Crash Course

As we indicated in the 13th edition of this book, the mission of this chapter is to provide you with the basic information that you need to survive in the constantly evolving world of collecting Americana. We considered omitting this section in this edition until we received a copy of your high school transcript, personality profile, and unpunched dance card from the Sweetheart Ball (which explained in full your picture in the yearbook).

The material that follows will assist you in planning and carrying out a road trip to the next antiques market on your schedule. Keep in mind that it has been prepared specifically for your needs and should *not* be shared with nonsubscribers.

Critical Information for Road Trips

Toll-Free Motel/Hotel Chain Telephone Numbers

Comfort Inns	800-228-5150
Days Inns	800-325-2525
Drury Inns	800-325-8300
Econo Lodges	800-55-ECONO
Fairfield Inns	800-228-2800
Hampton Inns	800-HAMPTON
Holiday Inns	800-HOLIDAY
Knights Inns	800-843-5644
La Quinta Motor Inns	800-531-5900
Ramada Inns	800-228-2828
Red Roof Inns	800-THE ROOF
Shoney's Inns	800-222-2222
Signature Inns	800-822-5252
Super 8 Motels	800-800-8000
Westin Hotels & Resorts	800-228-3000

Restaurants That Should Be on Your List

Herbert's Bar-B-Q
Franklin, TN

Located just off I-65 at exit 65 south of Nashville. An exceptional southern "bar-b-q" with the best corn bread we have ever eaten or experienced.

Ted's Jumbo Red Hots
2312 Sheridan Drive
Tonawanda, NY

Located off I-90 just east of Buffalo.

McDonald's
I-85 and Beatties Ford Road
Charlotte, NC

This McDonald's is a legendary soul-food cafeteria.

Mehlman Cafeteria
U.S. 40
St. Clairsville, OH

Located just off exits 220 or 218 of I-70 near Wheeling, WV.

Waffle House
5986 Financial Drive
Norcross, GA 30071
(404) 729-5700

There are Waffle Houses in 20 states in the west, midwest, and southeast. If there is a better franchised breakfast in America, we have yet to find it. The Norcross, Georgia, address will provide a brochure that lists the locations of Waffle Houses. Make it a point to try the hash browns scattered, smothered, covered, chunked, topped, and diced.

McGuire's Irish Pub & Brewery
Highway 98 (Gregory Street)
Pensacola, FL

Possibly serves the best French onion soup in the United States and a strong candidate for a world-class hamburger.

The Summit Diner
791 North Center Avenue
Somerset, PA
Exit 10 on I-90.

The Summit never closes and is a classic American diner with a menu listing exactly what you would expect.

Miller's Smorgasbord
Ronks, PA
Rt. 30 east of Lancaster, PA

Miller's has a smorgasbord that features a wide range of Pennsylvania-German foods. The pies they offer by way of UPS are the best you will ever get delivered.

Collector's Clubs

Collector's clubs put you in direct contact with individuals who share your specific interests. The newsletters are informative, pointing out shows, auctions, and publications that can enhance your collection and knowledge.

Old Sleepy Eye Collector's Club
Box 12
Monmouth, IL 64162

National Graniteware Society
P.O. Box 10013
Cedar Rapids, IA 52410

Schoenhut Collectors' Club
45 Louis Avenue
West Seneca, NY 14224

Catalog

Wurtsboro Wholesale Antiques
132 Sullivan Street
P.O. Box 386
Wurtsboro, NY 12790

We recommend ordering the Wurtsboro $2 illustrated catalog as a resource and reference tool to help in understanding the range of imported kitchen, hearth, and lighting items that frequently turn up in shops, shows, and markets.

Exceptional Antiques Shows

There are hundreds of antiques and collectibles shows and markets held in America each year. They range in quality from inspired to instilling a desire to perform a citizen's arrest on the individual selling admission tickets. We have chosen three inspired examples. To secure specific dates and information consult the advertisements in the *Maine Antiques Digest, Antique Review,* or *Antiques and the Arts Weekly.*

Dorset Antiques Festival
Dorset, VT
6 miles northwest of Manchester.
Held *every other* year in early July on the village green in Dorset (1995, 1997, etc.)

Heartland
Wayne County Fairgrounds
Richmond, IN
First Saturday in June

New Hampshire Antiques Dealers' Show
Manchester, NH
Usually held the second weekend in August at the Center of New Hampshire Holiday Inn

Antiques Markets

Antiques markets are growing in popularity among collectors and dealers because

a. They provide hundreds of booths filled with a wide range of merchandise in a single geographic setting over a brief time span (usually 1 or 2 days).

b. The inherent belief that somewhere in the massive display of merchandise and pile of humanity is the one item that will quench a lifelong quest.

c. They are relatively easy and economical for dealers to do and will bring thousands of potential customers.

We sincerely feel you need some direction when you attend an antiques market. For that reason we have put together the data that follows.

Accommodations

1. Don't assume that you can call a motel in the immediate area of the market a week before the event and secure a room. Well-established shows and markets have a following of collectors who reserve their rooms six months to a year in advance.

2. Telephone the local Chamber of Commerce and have them send you a list of motels and hotels within a 10-mile radius of the event. Take the time to inquire about local bed and breakfasts also.

3. The nationwide chains tend to fill up much more quickly than locally owned motels that don't have toll-free numbers.

Selecting a Vehicle

1. It is a given that you will find the precise piece of furniture you want when you arrive in a car rather than a station wagon or truck.

2. Take the largest vehicle that is available to you.

3. You will need packing materials to bring your purchases home. These include ropes, blankets, and rubber or fabric straps. The local hardware store in the town where the market is to be held *will be closed* or out of the items you need.

Parking

1. The key to parking at a market is to find some point of reference that will allow you to locate your vehicle on the way out.

2. Make it a point to find out early in the day the policy for driving into the market to pick up large purchases. Don't assume the dealers will know.

Dress

1. Assume the worst-possible weather scenario for the season and dress accordingly.

2. The shoes selected should be identical to those you wear to mow the lawn or work in the garden. Keep in mind that a fashion statement is not critical.

3. Include some inexpensive plastic rain wear as backup for the market experience. If you forget to bring rain gear, it *will* rain. You already have been assured the local hardware store and military surplus establishment will be closed.

Method of Payment

1. Large markets tend to draw exhibitors from a wide geographic area. Some dealers are hesitant to take checks and most do not accept credit cards.

2. Collectors who use cash often find transactions take place more quickly and many dealers create a "special" price for cash customers.

3. The standard questions of antiques consumers to dealers over the years have been:

a. What's your best price?
b. Is that the best you can do?
c. How much do you have to have for this?
d. What is the trade price?

When the medium of exchange is cash the question should be: What's the cash price?

Best Time to Arrive at the Market

1. There is absolutely no question that the key to success at most antiques markets is to get inside as quickly as possible.

2. Many markets and shows offer "early-bird" opportunities for collectors who want to pay $10–$40 above the normal gate fee to get into the show two or three hours before the general public. Usually this is a wise investment. Keep in mind that the majority of the dealers have shopped the event while booths were being set up prior to the early birds. Some markets allow the dealers and early birds to enter simultaneously, and the collectors make their purchases while the booths are being organized and the merchandise unpacked.

3. An alternative to the early bird or the regularly scheduled opening is to attend the market in its closing hours. This can create some interesting buying situations for the collector if there are dealers who have not had a good show, seriously need to sell something, or have a large cupboard or desk they would rather sell at cost than pack up and haul home.

Have a Plan

1. It is important to give some advance thought to the categories of antiques and collectibles in which you have special interest.

2. There is a tendency to have antiques tunnel vision. If you limit your interests to a specific item and concentrate your search on that, you may miss almost everything else at the market.

Dealing with Dealers

1. Don't automatically assume the dealers will have bags and wrapping materials for your purchases.

2. Carry a canvas tote bag filled with folded newspapers for wrapping your finds.

3. If you purchase something of even semi-consequence, get a receipt with the dealer's vital information on it.

4. If you encounter dealers who stock merchandise in which you have interest, pick up their business cards for future reference.

5. The price tag often carries a coded message as to how much the dealer will actually take for an item. Take a close look at it.

Food/Dining at the Market

1. At most markets the food tends to be predictable and the lines long.

2. Even though the food usually isn't very good, we have already given you eight places to eat on the way to the antiques market. You may have to drive out of your way, but you really have nothing to complain about.

CHAPTER THREE

Prices Past

Before we all begin the inevitable search for that great antiques market in the sky (never closes, takes checks, great food, no lines, deep discounts, valet parking), we want to give you an advance screening of the thrill your relatives can look forward to encountering at your estate auction.

Thirty or forty years down the dusty trail when many of us will be in a far better place, one of your relatives will casually pick this volume off a hay wagon at the auction. After briefly examining the frayed pages (from heavy consultation), the heir apparent will remark, "What a great book!" and immediately gather his/her sisters, brothers, spouses, and children to join in being mutually mystified and amazed that you didn't buy much more at such bargain prices in the 1990s.

We want to give you the opportunity to also revel in the past. To create that situation we have gone back through the previous 13 editions of this book and secured listings of auctions and antiques advertisements that stretch back to the 1920s. Take some time and look closely at the prices of Americana and wonder why your relatives didn't buy much more at such bargain prices.

Sixty-Five Pieces of Americana Offered for Sale, 1928–1954

June 1928

1. American oval walnut hutch table, **$25**
2. Bench table in pine, **$25**
3. Pine corner cupboard, 5'10" high × 28" across, refinished, **$150**

September 1928

4. American powder horns, **$6 each**
5. Iron candle snuffers, **$3**
6. Several good Windsors, **$25 and $30**
7. 1-drawer small maple candle stand, **$25**
8. Small maple and pine slope-top desk (very old), **$165**
9. Pine blanket chest, 1 long drawer, **$40**
10. 12-leg maple settee (deacon's bench), **$300**
11. Sailor's old pine chest, refinished, old hammered strap, **$50**
12. Old hickory bench, splendid condition, 74" long × 19" deep, 10 legs, **$100**
13. Old American pewter candlesticks, **$9 each**
14. Cobbler's candlestand, small, perfect, original, **$100**
15. Pine corner cupboard, butterfly shelves, **$27.50**
16. Pineapple high-post bed, **$275**

October 1928

17. Curly maple, 4 drawer chest, ball feet, old brasses, **$225**
18. Pine tavern table, c. 1720, **$95**
19. Maple slat-back arm chairs, 4 and 5 slats, **$12 each**
20. Queen Anne mirror, 42" × 23", **$1,000**

November 1930

21. Curly maple picture frames, 18" × 15", **$20**
22. Penna. comb-back Windsor armchair, **$200**
23. 8-leg pine table, refinished, **$75**
24. Rare Windsor rocker, knuckle arms, original, **$225**
25. Desirable old lowboy of cherrywood, **$150**
26. Curly maple highboy, sunburst top and bottom, old brasses, **$975**
27. Maple frames (not less than 25), **$1.50 each**
28. New England 9-room house, Revolutionary War Period, shipped anywhere in the U.S., disassembled, **$650**

July 1931

29. Richard Lee 8" pewter plate, **$35**
30. Fine walnut tavern table, cushion feet, **$85**

June 1932

31. Flintlock Ky. rifle, curly maple stock, **$20**

32. Set of 6 eagle splatted stenciled Hitchcock side chairs, **$360**

33. 3 Windsor fanback side chairs, **$105**

November 1933

34. A splendid little Franklin stove with andirons, **$68**

April 1934

35. Set of 6 decorated Hitchcock chairs, **$100**

36. Banjo clock with original painting and gilt bracket, **$175**

October 1934

37. Weathervanes: eagle, setter, cow, Pegasus, locomotive, **$20–$50**

38. Set of 6 Hitchcock chairs, crated, **$100**

June 1948

39. Wooden pitchforks, **$4.50 to $6.50**

40. Wooden grain scoops, **$4.50 and $7.50**

41. Conestoga wagon tar pot with lid, **$12.50**

August 1948

42. 2-wheel Enterprise coffee grinder, 24″ tall, diameter of wheel 17″, eagle finish, original condition, **$12.50**

43. Set of 30 alphabet blocks, various prints, **$8.50**

January 1949

44. Signed Shaker rocker, arms, original taped seat, **$32**

45. 6 plank-bottom Pennsylvania Dutch chairs, original stencil, **$195**

March 1949

46. Pair of Bennington Toby jugs, **$25**

April 1949

47. Large walnut corner cupboard, small paneled doors, spoon rack, **$200**

July 1949

48. Bird's-eye maple desk and chair, **$55**

December 1949

49. Curly maple table with birdcage, snake feet, 31¾″ diameter, **$165**

April 1954

50. 18th-century open pewter cupboard, oak, walnut and pine, 7′3″ high × 5′6″ wide, **$1,100**

51. Bennington Toby pitcher, **$8.50**

July 1954

52. 18th-century tin sconce with mirror, **$45**

53. Long-handled Pa. iron waffle iron, **$10**

54. 6 long-handled brass ladles, 2 with wrought iron handles, **$7 each**

55. Cherry candlestand, 17″ top × 28½″ tall, **$75**

August 1954

56. 18″ pewter charger, "John Jupe," c. 1750, **$32**

57. Dentist occupational shaving mug, owner's name in gold, "John A. Mies," **$25**

November 1954

58. 7 oval splat ladder-back chairs, **$100**

59. Scrimshaw whale's tooth, early sailing vessel with American flag, **$7.50**

60. Bennington ware pig bank, **$8.50**

61. Woven Pa. coverlet, red, white and blue, dated 1844, **$45**

62. Set of 28 graduated sleigh bells, range from 1¼″ to ¾″, **$65**

63. Powder flask, clasped hands and eagles, dated 1837, **$42.50**

64. Blanket chest, pine, painted blue, **$58**

65. Hired man's bed, red paint, **$35**

Shaker Antiques Auctions, 1972–1989

Sabbathday Lake, Maine, June 20, 1972

Two-door cupboard with clothespin pulls, 75″ high × 29″ wide × 14″ deep, **$700**

Henry Greene sewing desk with 12 drawers, Alfred, Maine, butternut and maple, 40½″ high × 31″ wide × 24″ deep, **$3,250**

Sabbathday Lake one-door cupboard used in dairy room, 53″ high × 26″ wide × 8½″ deep, **$275**

Mt. Lebanon, New York, Shaker Antiques, June 19, 1973

Revolver of swivel chair, 26″ high, chestnut, maple, and pine, **$1,000**

Pine, two-door panel end cupboard with five drawers, **$1,700**

No. 6 rocking chair with arms, **$125**

Bed with wooden rollers and traces of old green paint, **$625**

No. 7 signed rocking chair with cushion rail, **$255**

Lassiter collection in New York City, November 13, 1981

Benjamin Young tall case clock, **$26,000**

Curly maple side chair with tilters, **$4,180**

Pine cupboard, blind front, Mt. Lebanon, N.Y., **$12,500**

Pine and maple worktable with two drawers, Mt. Lebanon, N.Y., **$5,000**

Portland, Maine, May 27, 1983

Shaker sewing desk attributed to Elder Henry Greene, **$20,000**

Lady's cloak with hood, lining, and Sabbathday Lake label, **$525**

No. 7 rocking chair from Mt. Lebanon, N.Y., **$975**

Yellow painted miniature swift, Sabbathday Lake, **$60**

Postcards sold by the Shakers at various communities showing scenes of their daily lives, **$25 each**

Kingston, Massachusetts, June 12, 1983

Canterbury or Enfield, N.H., sewing desk, **$26,000**

Flax wheel signed "S.R.A.L.," Alfred, Maine, **$412.50**

Tailoring counter, **$2,860**

Small basket with slide lid, **$181.50**

New Lebanon, N.Y., cobbler's bench, **$3,630**

No. 6 slat-back armed rocking chair, Mt. Lebanon, N.Y., **$990**

Green 9″ oval box, **$715**

Rug beater with partial Mt. Lebanon label, **$104.50**

Natural finish 12″ oval box, **$247.50**

Refinished Mt. Lebanon footstool with label, **$275**

Duxbury, Massachusetts, June 30, 1984

Blue-gray blind-front cupboard with paneled door, 6′3½″ high, **$4,950**

Canterbury, N.H., side chair, original finish and tilters, **$2,200**

Sabbathday Lake blanket chest, original green paint, lift top with three drawers below, **$15,400**

Mt. Lebanon, N.Y., revolving chair in black paint, c. 1830, **$6,600**

Chrome yellow three-slat Watervliet rocking chair, **$1,540**

Pittsfield, Massachusetts, summer 1985

Production rocking chairs from Mt. Lebanon, N.Y.

No. 0 without arms, **$1,375**

No. 1 without arms, **$990**

No. 3 without arms (several were sold), **$440–$660**

No. 7 without arms, **$1,045**

No. 7 with arms, **$1,320**

Fitted sewing box with swing handle, **$385**

New Lebanon, N.Y., high chair, **$11,000**

Set of four rectangular butternut carriers, dovetailed sides, **$8,800**

Salmon painted chest, bracket base, four drawers, **$3,300**

Pittsfield, Massachusetts, August 6, 1989

No. 7 rocking chair with taped seat and back, **$990**

No. 0 child's rocking chair, **$1,650**

No. 6 armed rocking chair, **$1,100**

Chrome yellow oval box, 2½″ high × 3½″ long × 2½″ deep, pincushion on cover, **$8,800**

Framed string bean label, **$275**

Red painted blanket chest, **$2,200**

Shaker seed box, replaced lid, Mt. Lebanon label, **$1,540**

One Hundred Pieces from Garth's Auctions, 1975

1. Amber Coca-Cola bottle, Erie, Pa., **$6**

2. Tin cookie cutter, large rooster, **$22.50**

3. Tin cookie cutter, man with fat stomach, **$15**

4. Cast iron Aunt Jemima, **$15**

5. Wooden stocking stretchers, 38″ long, **$10**

6. Cast iron bank, circus lion, old gold, red, and blue paint, 5½″ high, **$35**

7. Copper candy kettle with iron handles and tripod stand, **$75**

8. Rare electric blue canning jar, 1 of 6 known, **$650**

9. Pine dovetailed ballot or ticket box, 11″ × 8″ × 8″, **$45**

10. Hanging pine knife scourer box, **$25**

11. Bird's-eye maple picture frame, 14½″ × 16¾″, **$85**
12. Bluebill drake decoy, central Wis., c. 1925, Yellow Lake, **$75**
13. Large copper candy kettle with iron handles, dovetailed, 18½″ diameter, **$75**
14. Wrought iron spatula, twisted handle, **$115**
15. Wrought iron and brass ladle and skimmer, signed, "F.B.S. Canton, O.," **$150**
16. Comb-back Windsor rocking chair, bamboo turnings, modern black paint, **$165**
17. Oval wooden bowl with handles, 20½″ long, **$45**
18. Knuckle-arm Windsor bench, curly maple base, shaped pine seat, curly maple arm supports and crest rail, refinished, **$1,200**
19. 4 Hitchcock-type side chairs, black with worn gold stenciling, **$120**
20. Primitive pine dough box, dovetailed and splayed base, dark red over other colors, **$55**
21. Sewer-tile frog, **$12.50**
22. Cracked butter mold, cased, sheaf of wheat, **$12.50**
23. Tin sander, **$8**
24. Tin cookie cutter of a woman, **$5**
25. Tin cookie cutter of a bear, **$5**
26. Tin cookie cutter of a chicken, **$13**
27. Tin Betty lamp and stand, **$125**
28. Two-section knife box with hinged lids, yellow combed decoration, 20th century, **$12.50**
29. Tin nutmeg grater, **$6**
30. Single cast-pewter candle mold, **$18**
31. Oval wooden bowl, refinished, 25½″ diameter, **$30**
32. Wooden sugar bucket with wire handle, **$25**
33. Burl mallet, **$10**
34. Hand-wrought double-edge ax with handle, 14″ long, **$20**
35. Poplar jelly cupboard, one-board doors, hinges replaced, old red paint, 45″ × 15″ × 47″ high, **$170**
36. Small rye basket, 6½″ diameter, **$7.50**
37. Blue calico print star cut from quilt, new painted frame, **$25**
38. Treen sand shaker, 7¼″ high, **$15**
39. Butter print, stylized tulips, 3½″ × 4¾″, **$75**
40. Wrought iron rushlight holder in wooden base, 13″ high, **$65**
41. Punched tin foot warmer, wooden frame with turned posts, **$45**
42. Cherry one-drawer nightstand, tapering legs, replaced top, **$85**
43. Brass sander, **$5**
44. Stoneware jug, stenciled ad for druggist, "Wheeling, W.Va.," **$25**
45. Iron double crusie lamp, twisted hanger, **$15**
46. Earthenware flowerpot, 9½″ high, **$20**
47. Noah's Ark, approx. 40 hand-carved animals, **$120**
48. Pair of wooden bellows with long flared brass nozzle, good leather, 34″ long, **$27.50**
49. A part of an early tombstone dated 1837, **$30**
50. Oval butter bowl, 23″ long, **$30**
51. Cast iron coffee grinder, Enterprise No. 5, 17″ high, worn original paint, **$190**
52. Cast iron matchbox, "Pat. 1872," **$20**
53. Wooden nutcracker, jaws of man in tricornered hat cracks the nut, **$7.50**
54. Wooden Conestoga wagon tar bucket, **$17.50**

55. Wooden apple peeler, **$40**

56. Tin ABC plate, "Who killed Cock Robin," **$17.50**

57. Primitive hearth broom, 43″ long, **$20**

58. Wooden baker's peel, 69″ long, **$25**

59. 3 gilded wooden letters "C.A.T.," 18″ high, **$55**

60. 2 wooden kitchen mashers, **$6**

61. Small poplar blanket chest, till, grained decoration, 38″ long × 19″ wide × 21″ high, **$105**

62. Pa. redware plate, wavy lines, old chips, 12½″ diameter, **$105**

63. Stoneware jar, stenciled "Greensboro Pa.," **$19**

64. Shaker wooden bootjack, **$30**

65. Wooden lemon squeezer, **$28**

66. Wooden 3-pronged hay fork, **$45**

67. Wooden shovel, 39″ long, **$45**

68. Wooden butter paddle, **$8**

69. Small copper funnel, battered end, **$5**

70. Tole apple tray, stenciled flowers, 11¾″ diameter, worn, **$40**

71. Set of 3 arrow-back side chairs, **$67.50**

72. Wooden cookie board, both sides have animal shapes, **$70**

73. Cast iron hitching post, 65″ high, **$75**

74. Blacksmith carry-all box, crude, **$17.50**

75. Skater's lantern, **$17.50**

76. Banjo, marked, "Pat. Jan. 4, '87," **$12.50**

77. Yellowware mixing bowl, blue stripe, 9¼″ di., **$5**

78. Signed iron broad axe, **$22.50**

79. Pine captain's chair, simple country turnings, refinished, **$30**

80. 4-tube tin candle mold, **$20**

81. Stoneware bottle, 9¼″ high, **$3**

82. American flag, 45 stars, 1896, 86″ × 140″, **$15**

83. Pine dry sink, refinished, paneled doors, 56″ long × 20″ wide × 45″ high, **$220**

84. 8-tube candle mold, tin, **$20**

85. Stoneware butter crock, embossed fruit and "Butter," 7″ diameter, **$27.50**

86. Copper wash boiler, polished, 27″ long, **$30**

87. Brass bed warmer with an incised floral design and turned handle, 43½″ long, **$170**

88. Wrought iron spatula, small size, 10¾″ long, **$20**

89. Brass dipper with wrought iron handle, 18″ long, **$80**

90. Early pine sawbuck table, 2-board top, 37″ × 92″ × 28½″, **$750**

91. Brass cigar cutter, polished, 18th century, **$27.50**

92. Tin 12-tube candle mold, **$33**

93. Tole bread box, green with black and yellow striping, clasp incomplete, **$5**

94. Early Colorado gold mine claim deed signed, "Richard Kellogg, Samson, Colo.," **$12**

95. Country hanging cupboard, one drawer and paneled door with applied heart, old blue-green paint, **$150**

96. Unusual granite ware preserving jar, 4¼″, **$20**

97. Iron safe with painted scene, key lock, on wheels, 10″ high, **$40**

98. Stoneware bottle, 10″ high, **$12**

99. Turned wooden pincushion, clamps to table top, **$40**

100. Large stoneware water jug, reddish brown glaze, 36″ high, 2 handles, **$70**

1670 Antiques Shop

(East Haverhill, Massachusetts, Magazine Advertisements)

January 1957

Tiny butter mold, cow's-head design, $5

Swan design butter mold, metal band, $3.50

17th-century wooden fish from a weathervane, $26

Flat-bottomed, roundish splint basket, 18″, $2.50

Fine 40″ butter scale, no paint, $45

Complete walnut spool cabinet, five drawers, $15

February 1957

Baby's rattle, tin, drum shape, whistle, $2

Rum swiggler, 5″ diameter, 4 iron bands, old blue paint, $5

March 1957

Marked iron porringer, 5½″, Kendrick, $7.50

Wooden butter stamp, sheep design, $9

E. G. Booz's Old Cabin Whiskey bottle, blue, $12.50

April 1957

Tin candle mold, 4 tubes, trays at both ends, $4.50

Round eagle butter stamp, nicely carved, $10

Wooden cookie roller with fish, fern, rabbit, $6

1702 Pennsylvania Dutch decorated smoothing board, $40

May 1957

Stout splint cheese basket, handle, 25″ diameter, $5

Wood butter stamp, cow design, long handle, $6

Red and blue homespun coverlet, 90″ × 99″, $25

December 1958

Eagle pattern blue and white homespun coverlet, $15

Hired man's bed, square posts with knobs, $12.50

Unusual early high chair, blue, rush seat, $17.50

Wood butter stamp, geometric leaf design, $1.50

Heavy wood plate or trencher, 8″, $12.50

Fancy cookie mold board, cat and dog, two-sided, $18

Brass skimmer, 6″, hand wrought, 15″ handle, $19

December 1968

Wooden kitchen spoon, 12″ long, $2.50

Staved sugar firkin or bucket, copper tacks, $12.50

Adjustable trammel, 31″ closed, lug pole hook, $20

Crudely carved cookie board, sailing ship, $22.50

Deep 13″ pewter charger, mended but good condition, $37.50

All-wood old-fashioned hinged lemon squeezer, $10

E. ROSS & CO   MFR   NO 95

CHAPTER FOUR

Interview with Opal Pickens

Over the past 25 years we have relied on the talents and knowledge of Opal Pickens of Watseka, Illinois. On numerous occasions we have asked her for a second opinion about the rarity or authenticity of a particular item we have tripped over in our travels. Invariably, Mrs. Pickens, who has been finding, buying, selling, and collecting Americana for more than 50 years, came through with a solution or suggestion for every question we raised.

We have called upon her years of experience one more time to assist us with this book and have posed some questions whose answers should be meaningful for all of us.

Q. How long have you been interested in antiques?

A. I have been a picker, dealer, and collector for more than 50 years.

Q. What is a picker?

A. A picker is a person who buys antiques from individuals, auctions, or shops and sells directly to dealers rather than the general public.

Q. How did you become a picker?

A. In the late 1930s my late husband Joe and I knocked on doors, attended farm auctions, and traveled extensively from Watseka, Illinois, to south of Terre Haute, Indiana, along both sides of the Illinois-Indiana border buying antiques.

Over the years we developed a route that we regularly took. Joe would take one side of the street in a small town or a group of houses around a grain elevator and I would take the other. These were difficult economic times and most people had things that had been in the family that they were willing to sell.

Q. How did you determine what you would pay for something?

A. We found out what the people were willing to sell, and the items we wanted were stacked on the kitchen table. We pulled out the three or four best items and paid the price we thought we would get when we sold them ourselves. We had no intention of making any profit on those things. For the six or eight other pieces, we usually made an offer that would give us a profit margin when we sold them to the dealers. We still had to leave the dealer some room for their profit.

The purpose of this method was that we wanted to come back and do business with these people again, so we were as fair with them as possible.

It's important to keep in mind that we didn't know what things were actually worth. We only knew what the dealers would pay us for a certain item. There were no price guides, magazines, or books that described the values of the kind of merchandise we were buying. It was a pretty instinctive business at this particular point in time.

Q. How many dealers did you sell to?

A. Keep in mind that there weren't as many dealers at that time as there are now. There were no antiques malls, and the shows were only held in the large cities. The people we sold to were general-line dealers who specialized in glass, jewelry, and Victorian furniture.

Q. What about the oak and pine furniture?

A. We saw oak tables, beds, and sets of chairs in almost every farmhouse. At the farm sales the oak was considered used furniture and very few people wanted it. It was impossible to sell oak to antiques dealers.

Most of the pine furniture had already been placed in the barns or outbuildings or on the back porch. That was fine with us because the pine is what we collected.

Q. Was there much interest in country furniture?

A. There was significant interest in early New England furniture that had been refinished, but it was hard to find even then. There were very few collectors of midwestern pine dry sinks, pie safes, or cupboards. The people who bought dry sinks made from local pine and poplar almost always stripped the painted finish down to the wood. Most of the dealers and collectors wanted walnut because that's what their parents and grandparents had had in their homes.

Q. How has the antiques business changed over the past 50 years?

A. It is a completely different world. Magazines, newspapers, and books are devoted to every type of antique and collectible. This has made people much more aware of value and the degree of rarity of everything. It also takes a great deal more knowledge to be successful today because 50 years ago we were much less concerned about reproductions and fakes.

The number of antiques shops has seriously declined and the number of collectibles malls has exploded. It seems that everyone has a tax number.

Fifty years ago it was a much more leisurely business and probably a lot more fun. Now it appears to me to be much more competitive and intense.

Q. What is the most unusual piece you ever purchased as a picker?

A. I don't know about the most unusual, but one day we were at a farmhouse in southern Indiana in the late 1930s. The family was moving to California, and everything in the house was for sale. They were only going to take their clothes, blankets, and some pots and pans. My husband bought two jars of marbles that had minimal value then but are highly collectible today. He bought them because nobody else wanted the marbles and he knew the family needed the money.

He never took the marbles out of the two jars and I still have them.

Three-gallon stoneware jug from New York State, 1870–1880. **$275–$325**

Front and back of rare butter print with decoration of American eagle and heart, hand carved, nineteenth century, 5½″ diameter. **$400–$500**

Butter scoop with hanging hook, maple, made from a single piece of wood, nineteenth century. **$250–$275**

Ovoid two-gallon jug with brushed capacity mark, 1830–1840, no maker's mark. **$175–$200**

Ovoid stoneware storage jar, c. 1840, 13″ tall. **$200–$235**

30

Swan butter mold, one-pound size, early twentieth century. **$135–$150**

Pennsylvania butter print, 3½" diameter, hand carved of maple, nineteenth century. **$225–$250**

Tin strainer, late nineteenth century. **$35–$50**

Turned maple funnel, 5½" diameter, New England in origin. **$75–$100**

Table or lap butter churn, midwestern in origin, unsigned and undecorated, late nineteenth century. **$150–$175**

31

Tole-decorated watering can with drop handle, late nineteenth century, American. **$200–$250**

Sponge-decorated pitcher, 8″ tall, 4″ diameter at base, unmarked, early twentieth century. **$150–$200**

Signed Bennington, Vermont, Rockingham pitcher, nineteenth century, some flaking at base. **$175–$300**

Molded stoneware milk pitcher, unsigned but probably White's, Utica, New York, late nineteenth century, 9″ tall. **$200–$240**

Sponge-decorated molded pitcher, 6" tall, early twentieth century. **$135–$175**

Molded stoneware pitcher, blue-and-white sponge decoration, unmarked, 10½" tall, early twentieth century. **$225–$275**

Painted fireplace bellows, pine, original condition, late nineteenth century. **$100–$135**

Mallet made of applewood, used to drive wooden pins into beams in barn construction, 5" diameter, nineteenth century. **$75–$85**

Sleepy Eye crock, early twentieth century, blue-and-gray molded stoneware, Monmouth, Illinois, pottery. **$400–$475**

Nineteenth-century foot stove, pine frame over pierced tin, drop handle. **$240–$300**

Oak splint utility basket, found in New York State. **$100–$125**

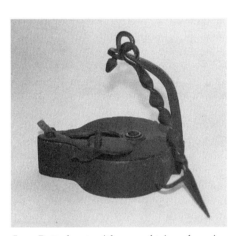

Iron Betty lamp with wrought-iron hanging hook, early nineteenth century, Pennsylvania. **$475–$525**

Redware apple-butter crock, applied handle, late nineteenth century, Pennsylvania origin, Albany slip interior. **$100–$135**

Gooseneck teakettle, copper, dovetailed bottom and drop handle, early nineteenth century. $300–$375

Saucer-based Betty lamp, tin, Pennsylvania, first half of the nineteenth century. $425–$500

Factory-made, saucer-based candleholder with storage tube for matches, original painted finish, late nineteenth century. $150–$175

Child's tin milk can for lunches, carved wooden stopper, late nineteenth–early twentieth century. $30–$40

Miniature cast-iron teakettle, early twentieth century, 6½" long × 7" to the top of the handle. $85–$95

Handcrafted oilcan with pouring spout, early twentieth century. $30–$40

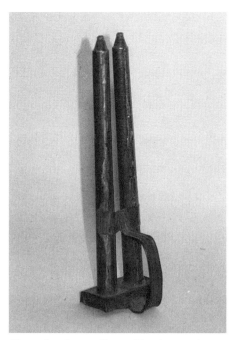

Six-tube tin candle mold, nineteenth century. $60–$70

Two-tube tin candle mold, nineteenth century, uncommon form. $135–$150

Rockingham-glazed pitcher, mid-nineteenth century, possibly Bennington, Vermont, in origin. **$150–$175**

American pewter teapot, nineteenth century. **$300–$400**

Unusual pine, hand-carved and -constructed spinning device, Pennsylvania in origin, early nineteenth century, refinished. **$325–$375**

Black cloth doll (**$175–$200**) and early twentieth-century homemade doll wagon, painted pine (**$65–$75**)

Painted pine doll chair, 14½" tall. **$85–$125**

37

Wheeled dog toy, early twentieth century, original condition, 7″ long tail to nose. $100–$140

Early twentieth-century Teddy bear, 8″ tall. $250–$325

Miniature keg, staved construction with iron bands, nineteenth century, drop handle, 7″ long, original unpainted surface. $95–$125

Ovoid three-gallon jug, unmarked and decorated, 1840s, kiln-damaged spout or mouth, probably a second at the pottery. $135–$150

Midwestern three-gallon jug with slip-trailed cobalt, no maker's mark, late nineteenth century. $80–$120

Three-gallon butter churn, no maker's mark, brushed floral decoration, 1860s–1870s. $375–$400

Refinished maple hand-carved dipper with handle designed for hanging, nineteenth century. $175–$225

Painted pine knife-and-fork box, splayed sides, carved handle, mid-nineteenth century. $135–$175

Redware bank, Albany slip glaze, 1880s, Pennsylvania. $150–$175

Cast flat iron, mid-nineteenth century. $100–$125

Machine-impressed wheat butter stamp, 5½" diameter. $95–$115

African-American doll, 15" tall, composition head, 1930s. $325–$385

Metal advertising piece from the National Fire Insurance Co., used to mark ledger pages and to tear receipts, c. 1905, original condition. $75–$100

Hand-carved dipper, maple, original unpainted finish, nineteenth century, 13" long, American. $200–$275

40

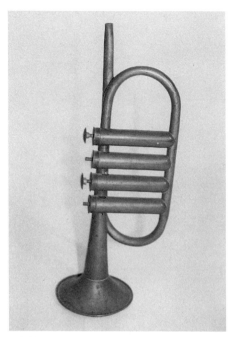

Child's musical instrument, c. 1920, 11″ long. $25–$35

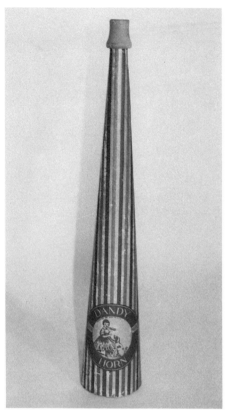

Child's paper-covered horn, red, white, and blue stripes, 1930s. $20–$25

Unusual pair of open-weave child's leather shoes, c. 1910. $50–$55

Horse pull toy on wheeled pine platform, 1920s, German origin. $240–$300

Texie cigar box, original condition. $100–$125

Cow pull toy on wheeled pine platform, 1920s, replaced horns. $200–$235

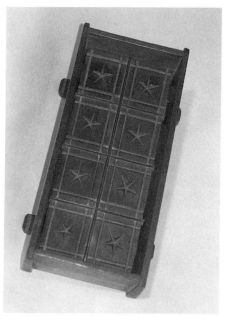

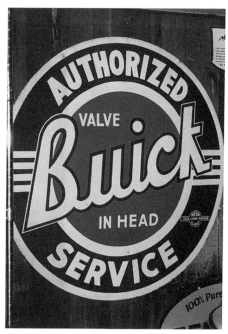

Butter mold in rectangular box, maple, machine-impressed designs, 14″ × 6″, early twentieth century. $225–$275

"Authorized Buick Service" metal sign, 48″ diameter, 1940s. $400–$485

Copper pan, 11" diameter, nineteenth century, probably European in origin. **$50–$65**

Schoenhut white horse, 1920s, painted eyes. **$225–$240**

Cast-brass horse-blanket pin, late nineteenth century, 7" long. **$30–$35**

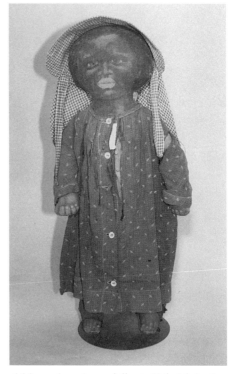

Nickel-over-copper teakettle, early 1900s. **$45–$55**

African-American doll, stuffed fabric face and body, original clothing, 1920s. **$350–$400**

Dog pincushion, early 1900s. $55–$60

Windup walking camel toy, 1940s, 7½″ long. $75–$85

Maple rolling pin with carved molds for cookies, late nineteenth century. $150–$175

Shoe pincushion, fabric with leather heel, early 1900s. $45–$55

Child's dress, hand made, c. 1915. $100–$150

44

Molded cardboard Easter rabbit candy container, 1930s–40s. **$60–$75**

Molded cardboard Easter rabbit candy container, 1930s–40s. **$60–$75**

Gold Edge Blend Roasted Coffee bin, painted red with gold lettering, early 1900s, 20″ wide × 36″ tall × 18″ deep. **$200–$285**

Child's high chair, in salmon paint, late nineteenth century, pine and maple, minor repairs. **$175–$250**

45

CHAPTER FIVE

The Schoenhut Humpty Dumpty Circus

Between 1903 and 1935 the A. Schoenhut Company of Philadelphia, Pennsylvania, manufactured a staggering variety of toys that ranged from pianos to sailboats. The Humpty Dumpty Circus is probably the Schoenhut product best remembered by Americana collectors today.

The simple 1903 set that included a ladder, chair, and clown evolved into combinations of animals, performers, and equipment, and eventually even a tent to use when putting on a miniature performance that rivaled the Ringling Brothers.

Key Dates for Collectors

Mid–1860s—Albert Schoenhut came to the United States and was operating a toy factory in Philadelphia in 1872. Schoenhut died in 1912.

Lady circus rider with bisque head. **$350–$450**

Lady circus rider with wooden head and painted eyes. **$350**

1903—The Humpty Dumpty Circus was introduced in 1903. The set consisted of a chair, clown, and ladder. Eventually the clowns were dressed in fabric of more than 20 different designs. Before the decade was over the circus had grown to include a tent, circus wagons, a wide variety of equipment, and numerous animals and performers.

1906—The Humpty Dumpty Circus tent was initially marketed in 1906.

1918—Prior to 1918 the animals were made with glass eyes. After that date the eyes were painted. Before World War I the ringmaster, lady acrobat, and lady circus rider were available with bisque heads. The conflict in Europe apparently forced Schoenhut to substitute molded wooden heads.

1923—A reduced-size version of the circus appeared in 1923, complete with a scaled-down tent.

1929—The Schoenhut circus was extensively advertised in a variety of popular and trade publications until 1929. An early advertisement appeared in the November and December 1903 issues of *Ladies Home Journal* and such ads continued for many years at Christmas time. The hard times brought on by the Great Depression may have been a factor in Schoenhut's decision to halt most print-media advertising.

1932—In 1928 and 1932 two additional circus tents were offered to the general public. These rectangular tents are rarely seen by collectors today.

1935—The Schoenhut Company, which found it impossible to profitably conduct business during the economic disaster in the United States, closed forever in 1935.

Ringmaster with wooden head and painted eyes. $400

Lion tamer with red felt fez, molded wooden head, and painted eyes. $475

Questions and Answers

Judith Lile is one of the nation's most respected and knowledgeable antique toy dealers. Her special interest is the products of the A. Schoenhut Company of Philadelphia, Pennsylvania, creators and marketers of the Humpty Dumpty Circus.

Ms. Lile does an extensive mail-order business from 346 Valleybrook Drive, Lancaster, PA 17601, and can be reached by telephone at (717) 569-8175. She also has a booth (#130) at the Black Angus Antique Mall in Adamstown, Pennsylvania. The Black Angus is open each Sunday from 8 A.M. to 5 P.M.

Q. How did you initially become interested in the Humpty Dumpty Circus?

A. When I went into the business of selling antique toys (leaving a career as an English teacher), I bought the collection of a friend who was a well-established toy dealer. Her inven-

tory ranged from 1930s tin windups to early cloth dolls to German stables to a large Humpty Dumpty circus. Though I was more attracted at first to the elegant paper-lithographed doll houses, I shortly began to notice the charm of the Schoenhut animals and people. As collectors came into my booth to look at them, I saw how different aspects appealed to different people, how some pieces were valued for their form or paint while others offered a certain winning expression. I saw that each piece had its own quality and interest, and soon I had gone from "not competing with my customers" to being an enthusiastic Schoenhut collector and dealer.

Q. Which of the personnel are the most difficult to find?

A. The rarest personnel are probably those belonging to the Teddy Roosevelt set. Made only from 1909 to 1911, the figures are very scarce. Teddy himself turns up occasionally, but the photographer, the naturalist, the taxidermist, the doctor, etc., are very seldom in circulation. Arguably just as rare are the Style I, two-part head lady and gent acrobats, and, after these, the two-part head lion tamer and ringmaster.

Q. What are among the rarest of the circus animals?

A. Among the animals, those made for the Teddy Roosevelt set are also extremely rare—the glass-eyed hyena, zebu, gazelle, and gorilla. But the rarest of all the animals are from the farm set—the glass-eyed cat, rabbit, and wolf. The hardest-to-find circus animals are the carved-mane glass-eyed lion and buffalo, two-humped glass-eyed camel, glass-eyed polar bear, and kangaroo.

Some seemingly common animals are the most sought-after. The glass-eyed white horse, for example, is extremely popular, as are the giraffe, the leopard, the elephant with blanket and howdah, and the tiger. The common farm animals—the cow and the lamb—are also in demand along with the uncommon milkmaid and Mary.

Q. How difficult to find are the circus tents?

A. The full-sized tents turn up occasionally but often not in good condition. The flags, banners, trapeze bar, and rings are sometimes missing and the canvas discolored or torn. On the other hand, fine examples have also survived as part of well-cared-for collections. My own inventory has averaged about one good tent per year. The reduced-size tents, made into the early 1930s, are more common and usually in better condition. A full-size tent in excellent and complete condition would probably cost between $2,000

and $2,400, and a reduced-size one between $1,000 and $1,200.

Other structural accessories are more difficult to find than the tents: the flexible cage, the horizontal bar, the tight rope, the seesaw. These simply made items bring relatively high prices because of their scarcity.

Q. Is there a piece of Schoenhut that you have searched for and never found?

A. I collect the Teddy Roosevelt set, two-part-head people, and two-part-head clowns. The hardest to find have been the Teddy Roosevelt personnel. I have Teddy and the African chief, but the others remain elusive. I also have the early wild animal-cage wagon with the horses and driver. That's my favorite piece.

Q. Do more collectors prefer the full-size animals and personnel or the reduced-size?

A. Most collectors prefer the regular-size circus to the reduced-size. There is much more hand carving and painting on the earlier pieces, giving them greater force and individuality. The reduced-size circus, however, has a simple charm that many collectors appreciate.

Q. How important is condition in determining value of Schoenhut animals and personnel?

A. Though some collectors enjoy the look of age and play, the value of a Schoenhut piece is determined by its condition. First, the overall paint: Is there much wear? Many scrapes or nicks? Gouging at the nail holes from improper restringing? Then the parts: Are the ears, tail, or horns still

The more common one-part head clowns in excellent condition start at about $150. Earlier clowns generally cost more.

on? Are they original? In decent shape? In general, minor repairs, while affecting the full value of a piece, are usually accepted if they're skillfully done. The Humpty Dumpty circus was made to be played with and finding these toys in mint or near-mint condition is the exception rather than the rule.

Q. Do replaced costumes have a significant effect on the value of the personnel?

A. Collectors look for an original and complete costume: Hat, jacket, tie, petticoat, gold paste or ric-rac. They look also for fabric in good condition with good color. There are often moth holes in the felt clothing. These aren't considered serious (if they're small) and can be left as is or "pieced out" with old felt without really greatly reducing the value. A replaced costume, however, devaluates the piece significantly. Note: Schoenhut clowns (made from 1903 to the early 1930s) came in approximately twelve variations in almost twenty different costumes. Serious collectors are urged to find a copy of *Schoenhut's Humpty Dumpty Circus from A to Z* by Evelyn Ackerman and Frederick Keller (Era Industries, Inc., Los Angeles, 1975).

Circus Pieces

Personnel

chinaman acrobat
clown
gent acrobat
hobo

lady acrobat
lady rider
lion tamer
Negro dude
ringmaster

52

Reduced-Size Personnel

clown
hobo
lady rider
Negro dude
ringmaster

Animals

alligator
brown bear
buffalo
bulldog
burro
camel, Arabian
camel, Bactrian
cat
cow
deer
donkey
elephant
gazelle
giraffe
goat
goose
gorilla
hippopotamus
horse, dark
horse, white
hyena
kangaroo
leopard
lion
monkey
ostrich
pig
polar bear
poodle
rabbit
rhinoceros
sea lion
sheep
tiger
wolf
zebra
zebu

Poodle with cloth mane and glass eyes. **$400**

53

Painted-eye poodle with molded head. **$200**

Glass-eyed tiger. **$700**

Painted-eye tiger with molded head. **$450**

Painted-eye leopard with molded head (reduced size). **$350**

Giraffes with molded heads and painted eyes, short horns made from wooden dowels, and woven cord tails. **$400**

Goat with painted eyes, five-pointed leather tail and whiskers, leather ears and horns. **$325**

Painted-eye Bactrian (two-humped) camel with molded head. **$375**

Extra-fine elephant with glass eyes, howdah blanket, and triangular headdress. **$275–$375**

Painted-eye elephant with leather ears, twine tail, and rubber trunk extension. **$175**

Regular (**$175**) and reduced-size (**$100**) elephants with painted eyes.

Brown bear with leather tail and ears, dark chocolate paint. **$450**

Painted-eye donkey with twine tail, leather ears, and black cloth mane. **$125**

Lion with painted eyes, molded wooden head, and a tail made of twisted twine. **$350**

Dark horse with painted eyes, molded head, leather ears, black hooves, and black-thread tail. **$225**

White horse with painted eyes, molded head, and wooden disk platform. **$225**

Monkey with molded head, painted eyes, red felt costume and hat. **$500**

Reduced-Size Animals

(The reduced-size circus animals all have painted eyes.)
brown bear
buffalo

camel, Bactrian
donkey
elephant
giraffe
goat

hippopotamus
horse, dark
horse, white
leopard
lion
ostrich
pig
poodle
rhinoceros
tiger
zebra

Equipment and Accessories

ball
barrel
bottle with label
cane

chair
flag
flexible cage
goblet
hoop
horizontal bar
ladder
parasol
pedestal, short
pedestal, tall
ring
seesaw
table
tightrope
tub, solid color
tub with paper bands
weights (50 lbs., 100 lbs., 200 lbs.)
whip

Ladder. $12–$20

Chairs and table. $15–$20

White table. $20

Two sizes of chairs. $15–$20

Painted tub decorated with a colorful paper strip. $25

Pedestals decorated with painted stripe or strips of paper. $20–$28

Reduced-size Humpty Dumpty Circus tent. **$1200–$1500**

Painted balls made from three pieces of wood. $15–$20

Painted barrel. $20

Full-size Humpty Dumpty Circus tent. **$1500–$2200**

Evaluating Schoenhut Circus Toys

Attempting to develop a price guide for Schoenhut circus personnel and animals can get unusually complex because of the combinations and varieties of styles, open and closed mouths, glass and painted eyes, and other deviations from the norm too numerous to discuss.

For our purposes, the animals and personnel listed will be:

1. In excellent condition, which is defined as animals or personnel with original paint and wood showing signs of wear from play, with minimal flaws but no serious damage. Costumes, saddles, bridles, ears, tails, etc., can be slightly soiled but intact and not damaged or replaced.

2. The *most common* example as to style, color, and painted eye/glass eye that a collector may encounter.

Keep in mind that examples of animals or personnel that are an unusual style variation and are in excellent condition are going to be worth *more* than the *most commonly found* examples priced here.

Set No. 15/1, 4 pieces, 50 cents
Weight 15 ozs

Set No. 20/3, 7 pieces, $1.25
Weight 2 lbs.

Set No. 20/16, 7 pieces, $2.25
Weight 3 lbs. 14 ozs.

Set No. 20/1, 3 pieces, $1.00
Weight 1 lb. 12 ozs.

EXTRA FINE
Set No. 20/26, 15 pieces, $4.00
Weight 6 lbs. 12 ozs.

Set No. 20/7, 5 pieces, $1.50
Weight 2 lbs. 11 ozs.

Set No. 20/22, 10 pieces, $3.00
Weight 3 lbs. 3 ozs.

Set No. 20/21, 11 pieces, $3.00
Weight 4 lbs. 6 ozs.

EXTRA FINE
Set No. 20 31, 22 pieces, $6.00
Weight 8 lbs. 7 ozs.

Circus Ring

Splendid Accessory to the Humpty Dumpty Circus

Frame and Ring made of wood and nicely painted

THE HUMPTY DUMPTY CIRCUS

This Circus Ring adds greatly to the enjoyment of the Humpty Dumpty Toys, as it helps to make them more real and circus like.

No. 30 1. $1.00.
Size, 24 ¼ x 24 ¼.   Weight, 5 lbs.

PRICE GUIDE TO SCHOENHUT ANIMALS

| ANIMAL | REGULAR SIZE | | REDUCED SIZE |
	PAINTED EYES	GLASS EYES	
alligator	$345	$550	
brown bear	450	650	$450
buffalo	350	650*	400
bulldog	900	1,600	
burro	350	450	
camel, Arabian (one hump)	375	600	
camel, Bactrian (two hump)	375	1,600	400
cat	1,500	4,000	
cow	500	800	
deer	700	950	
donkey	125	175	100
elephant	175	275	100
gazelle	1,000	2,000	
giraffe	400	600	400
goose	450		
gorilla	400		
hippopotamus	400	600	450
horse, dark	225	400	150
horse, white	225	400	150
hyena	1,800	3,500	
kangaroo	850	1,350	
leopard	450	700	350
lion	350	650*	350
monkey	500		
ostrich	500	700	600
pig	375	500	600
polar bear	900	1,800	
poodle	200	400*	500
rabbit	750	4,000	
rhinoceros	450	650	425
sea lion	675	950	
sheep	500	750	
tiger	450	700	350
wolf	1,000	4,000	
zebra	400	700	425
zebu	1,600	4,000	

*Prices for the glass-eyed buffalo, lion, and poodle refer to the *cloth-maned* style.

PRICE GUIDE TO SCHOENHUT PERSONNEL*

Chinaman	$550
clown	150
gent acrobat	1,000
hobo	400
lady acrobat	450
lady circus rider	350
lion tamer	475
Negro dude	500
ringmaster	400

*Prices of personnel refer to the later, one-part head pieces. Earlier styles are generally higher priced.

CHAPTER SIX

Decorated Stoneware

Fakes and Reproductions

Recently we have read several articles in antiques publications that warned collectors about the growing concerns about early salt-glazed stoneware crocks and jugs with contemporary decoration. In an earlier edition of this book, the tale of a nineteenth-century jug with the detailed caricature of an American Indian was related by the man who purchased it for a bargain price at auction. He wrote a letter to us in an attempt to secure an opinion about its authenticity and sent along several photographs.

A cursory glance at the photographs would have probably suggested to the most casual of stoneware collectors that the jug was legitimately nineteenth century in origin but the decoration was added almost a full century later.

The procedure in faking cobalt decoration of previously undecorated nineteenth-century stoneware is relatively simple. Undecorated salt-glazed jugs are still available and are relatively inexpensive. Newly executed cobalt slip-decorated birds, deer, or scenes are added and the piece is refired. Occasionally, blue permanent marking pens are used rather than the more labor-intensive cobalt slip.

The second technique is to offer antiques collectors contemporary pieces of decorated stoneware originally produced by legitimate potters as reproductions but later modified by removing incised or impressed marks. These altered pieces are then offered as early wares on the secondary market. These contemporary pieces tend to be considerably lighter in weight than nineteenth-century examples and also feel different to the touch.

It is important at this point to note the similarities in the manner bogus decorated stoneware and baseball memorabilia are marketed by individuals intent on deception and significant profits. Collectors of game-worn major league baseball uniforms normally don't have to worry about fakes when they purchase the 1993 road uniform of a third-string catcher with the Texas Rangers. The profit margin is so low on a $125 jersey that there is no motivation to reproduce it. It is equally as labor intensive to make the jersey appear to be one worn by a budding superstar, but it is dramatically more profitable.

The process involved in faking a piece of decorated stoneware is identical. To take a $50 nineteenth-century undecorated jug, add a contemporary cobalt flower, and sell it for $125 is foolish. The tendency is for faked decoration to be much more elaborate and offered for hundreds or thousands of dollars. A house, horse, or detailed bird on a branch is the more typically faked decoration as opposed to hastily drawn insects, geometric lines, or inverted Christmas trees. The profit margin is significantly greater and the amount of work is almost identical.

Stoneware pieces with newly executed cobalt decoration require some marketing strategy when offered for sale. Dealers in fakes usually offer one piece at a time in selected venues. If three or four similarly decorated pieces suddenly turn up at the same auction, show, or market, people begin to take notice to a much greater degree than is the case with a single isolated example.

The point of this discussion is obvious: Collectors should take special pains to examine exceptional examples of decorated stoneware. They are the pieces that tend to be faked because they are the most valuable. While collectors today should be concerned and aware of the possibility of newly decorated stoneware in the marketplace, it is not necessary to question or automatically assume every piece of consequence is "wrong." The key is to buy intellectually rather than emotionally from dealers in whom you can place your trust.

Notes for Collectors

1. Stoneware collectors generally evaluate stoneware on the basis of the following criteria:

   a. decoration
   b. condition
   c. maker's mark
   d. form

2. The more sophisticated or detailed the decoration of a piece of stoneware, the greater the willingness of most collectors to accept cracks, flaking, or chips.

3. The interest in collecting regional pottery is continuing to become more intense in specific geographic areas as exceptional pieces increasingly become harder to locate. For example, pieces from Edgefield, S.C., or Anna, Illinois, have more value in the southeast or midwest where they were produced than in any other section of the nation.

   A heavily decorated New York State or New England churn with double cobalt birds on a log is consistently in demand and people are willing to pay comparable prices throughout the United States. There are minimal geographic or economic influences on heavily decorated nineteenth-century stoneware.

4. We still stand by the comment made in previous editions that the best source for decorated stoneware is dealers who specialize in this type of ware. They understand the market and price their wares accordingly.

5. When you purchase a piece of stoneware, it is essential that you secure a receipt that accurately describes its age, decoration, maker, and condition. Have the seller sign and date the receipt and add his/her address and telephone number.

Stoneware at Auction

Vicki and Bruce Waasdorp have conducted semi-annual decorated-stoneware auctions by mail and telephone for several years. Prior to each auction the Waasdorps issue a fully illustrated catalog for collectors to study. Each piece of stoneware offered for sale in the auction is pictured and described in detail.

Collectors may use the mail, fax, or telephone to make their bids within a specific time frame. Following the auction, each subscriber to the catalog receives a listing of the prices realized at auction.

Information may be secured by contacting:

Vicki and Bruce Waasdorp
P.O. Box 434
10931 Main Street
Clarence, NY 14031
(716) 759-2361

The pictures, descriptions, and prices that follow were provided by the Waasdorps from their October 2, 1994, mail and telephone auction.

Crocks, C.W. Braun, Buffalo, New York, c. 1880. Left: *Two-gallon, very minor stain spots,* **$120.** Right: *Five-gallon with wreath, excellent condition,* **$120.**

Crocks, J. Fisher, Lyons & Co., Lyons, New York. Left: *Two-gallon with fern decoration, excellent condition,* **$250.** Right: *Three-gallon with brushed leaf design, excellent condition, c. 1880,* **$325.**

Unsigned three-gallon crock with detailed star design, professional restoration to tight line in the side, 10" tall, c. 1870. **$650**

E.B. Norton, Worcester, Massachusetts, three-gallon crock with dark blue parrot on plume, replaced right ear and restoration to extensive lines in back, c. 1870. **$270**

N.A. White & Son, Utica, New York, four-gallon crock with paddletail and plume decoration, professional restoration to both rim chip and Y-shaped crack in back, c. 1885. **$700**

"Union Pottery, J. Zipp, Prop. New Jersey," four-gallon crock, dated "1888," 6" tight through line in front, 1" hairline in back. $280

S.D. Kellogg, Whately, three-gallon crock with large floral design, rare mark, minor glaze pitting at the base. **$240**

A.E. Smith & Sons Manufacturers, Peek Slip, New York, two-gallon crock with thick brush-stroke design, minor age spider on the side, c. 1870. **$140**

One-gallon crocks, Lyons, c. 1860. Left: Brushed flower design, minor surface chip at base in back, **$190.** Right: Ovoid with simple leaf design, excellent condition, **$180.**

N.A. White & Son, Utica, New York, two-gallon crock with orchid decoration, c. 1885.
$190

John Burger, Rochester, New York, five-gallon crock with large, detailed fern decoration, tight 4" line near front and in back, c. 1855.
$800

Burger & Lang, Rochester, New York, six-gallon crock with large slip-decorated daisy, long tight stabilized hairline in back, c. 1870.
$500

N. Clark, Jr., Athens, New York, two-gallon crock with flower, minor glaze line at base, c. 1850. **$130**

J.S. Taft & Co., six-gallon crock with stylized decoration, 5" tight crack in side, c. 1870. Estimated value: **$180–$270**

Unsigned three-gallon crock with large robin, professional repairs to freeze lines on front and base and rim chip repairs, c. 1870. **$230**

J. Burger, Jr., Rochester, New York, three-gallon crock with fern wreath design, excellent condition, c. 1885. **$300**

Whites, Utica, New York, four-gallon crock with running bird, professional restoration to glaze flaking on side and rear, glued chip on side and minor hairlines in rim, c. 1865. **$300**

Harts, Fulton, New York, five-gallon crock with exceptional dotted and ribbed dog, minor glaze spider in front, very tight 5" hairline in back, c. 1860. **$5000**

Unsigned three-gallon advertising crock with blue script on front and a slip-decorated bird on the other side, rim chip above one ear and age spider, both minor, c. 1885. **$600**

Burger & Lang, Rochester, New York, five-gallon crock with huge dark blue poppy, professional repairs to rim chips and to line in front, c. 1870. **$400**

T. Harrington, Lyons, New York, four-gallon crock with large dotted bird on a log, 8" tight stabilized crack, otherwise excellent condition, c. 1855. **$5250**

Haxstun Ottman & Co., Fort Edward, New York, one-gallon jug with bird, excellent condition, c. 1870. **$500**

Harrington & Burger, Rochester, New York, two-gallon jug with vivid sunflower, very minor design fry & stack mark, c. 1852. **$725**

J. Burger, Jr., Rochester, New York, two-gallon jug with slip-decorated daisy, c. 1885. **$280**

J. Clark & Co., Troy, New York, "Bristols Beer" and embossed eagle on front, three-gallon double-handled cooler, professional repair to minor chip in relief design, one-year mark, c. 1826. **$2100**

New York Stoneware Co., Fort Edward, New York, one-gallon jug with long-tailed bird, excellent condition, c. 1870. $675

J. Seymour, Troy, New York, three-gallon jug with peacock and leaf design, rim chip on spout, minor stack mark in the making and 6" tight through line just touching design on left, c. 1855. $1800

Thompson & Tyler, Troy, New York, one-gallon jug with geometric design, chip at base, excellent condition, c. 1859. $230

E.E. Hall & Co. advertising jug with slip-decorated bird, minor glaze lines from age, c. 1870. $425

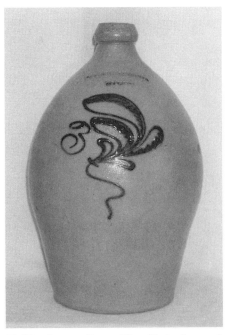

T. Harrington, Lyons, New York, three-gallon ovoid jug with leaf design, glued stabilized crack in handle and minor stone ping, c. 1855. $230

Lyons three-gallon jug with large ribbed flower, excellent condition, c. 1855. $625

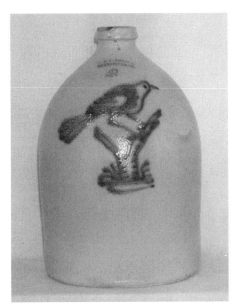

J. & E. Norton, Bennington, Vermont, two-gallon jug with bird on stump, chip at spout, c. 1855. $1600

W.H. Farrar, Geddes, New York, one-gallon jug with finely detailed bird and sunflower, a few insignificant glaze flakes, c. 1860. $5750

Unsigned three-gallon ovoid jug with incised and blued flower and leaf, attributed to Clarkson Crolius, New York, c. 1795. **$3200**

E.A. Buck & Co., one-gallon advertising pouring jug, chip in spout, 5″ tight crack in side, c. 1870. **$90**

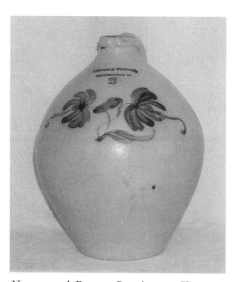

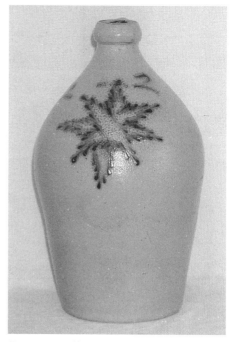

Norton and Fenton, Bennington, Vermont, two-gallon ovoid jug, spout chips, c. 1845. **$725**

Lyons two-gallon ovoid jug with star design, professional restoration to minor stone ping, c. 1855. **$200**

Ithaca, New York, one-gallon ovoid crock with slip-decorated parrot, tight 5" Y-shaped through line on side and minor line in base in front, c. 1865. $325

Whites, Utica, New York, three-gallon jar with vivid cobalt orchid, c. 1865. $270

T. Harrington, Lyons, New York, three-gallon jar or tabletop churn, closed tulip design, professional repair to a few tight lines from use, c. 1855. $675

Lyons, New York, one-gallon preserve jar with brush blue decoration, 1" rim line on side, otherwise excellent condition, c. 1860. $170

Unsigned two-gallon preserve jar with crisp dark blue Bennington-type design, professional restoration to minor rim chip, c. 1860. $210

Unsigned three-quart batter pail attributed to Whites, Utica, New York, factory, pine tree design and bail handle, excellent condition, c. 1865. $525

Left: Cowden & Co., Harrisburg, Pennsylvania, one-gallon milk pan in a white bristol glaze, minor rim chip in back, c. 1880, estimated value, $60–$80. Right: Unsigned two-gallon cake crock with slip decoration, midwest origin, base chips and a stack mark in the making, c. 1880, estimated value, $140–$210.

Unsigned Cortland half-gallon jar with blue floral decoration, flaking on bottom of crock, minor tight hairline in back, c. 1860. $325

Cortland, New York, one-gallon jar with double bellflower design, very minor age spider, c. 1860, very rare script "B" in cobalt. **$375**

C.W. Braun, Buffalo, New York, one-gallon ovoid crock with slip-decorated bird on branch, c. 1860. **$550**

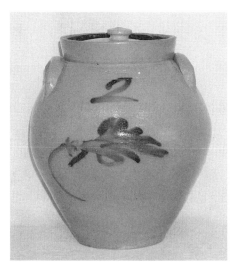

N. Clark & Co., Mt. Morris, New York, two-gallon ovoid jar with original lid, brush-decorated "2" and blue plume, base chip, minor glaze spiders and rim chips in back, c. 1840. **$350**

T. Crafts, four-gallon ovoid preserve jar with brush blue accents, original lid, uncommonly large size for a jar, minor age crazing in the glaze, c. 1835. **$280**

J. & E. Norton, Bennington, Vermont, four-gallon jar with crossed peacocks on a tree, professional restoration to insignificant line on the side, c. 1855. $5500

Lyons two-gallon preserve jar with brushed decoration, repair to rim chip and stone ping in the making, 12" tall, c. 1860. $270

Highly decorated blind pig keg, possibly Pennsylvania, minor age spiders in base and near bung hole, 9" tall, c. 1850. $1450

C. Dillon & Co., Albany, New York, two-gallon ovoid crock, uncommon two-year mark, stone ping on side, nice form, 11" tall, c. 1834. $140

J. Burger, Jr., Rochester, New York, five-gallon ovoid crock with large partridge, uncommon ovoid form for a crock this large, minor rim chip in back, c. 1885. **$2000**

L. Norton & Son four-gallon ovoid crock with ochre decoration, professional restoration to line in the front and stone ping in the making, uncommon mark, c. 1835. **$230**

J. Heiser, Buffalo, New York, two-gallon preserve jar with elaborate floral design, professional repairs to rim chip in front and line on the side, c. 1852. **$200**

Lyons two-gallon preserve jar with bright blue double tulip decoration, repaired rim chip, 12" tall, c. 1855. **$400**

Left: *Unsigned, approximately one-gallon jar, flowers surrounding the entire piece, chip at base and insignificant rim chips, probably Pennsylvania or Maryland origin, c. 1840,* **$230.** Right: *Unsigned, approximately half-gallon cake crock, arrows surrounding the diameter, through line across diameter and up both sides, c. 1850,* **$120.**

Left: *Unsigned ovoid jar with brush blue accents, rim chip in front and back, probably New York in origin, 12" tall, c. 1835. Estimated value,* **$100–$150.** Right: *Unsigned ovoid crock with brush blue accents, very minor pock mark in the making, probably New York in origin, c. 1840,* **$200.**

Lyons, New York, two-gallon preserve jar with brushed decoration, repair to rim chip and stone ping in the making, 12" tall, c. 1860. **$100**

Cowden & Wilcox, Harrisburg, Pennsylvania, two-gallon butter pail with elaborate floral decoration, a few insignificant chips from use, 10½" tall, c. 1870. **$1550**

Hastings & Belding, Ashfield, Massachusetts, two-gallon preserve jar with original lid, only a four-year mark, rim chip and minor glaze lines, c. 1851. **$150**

N.A. White & Son, Utica, New York, five-gallon churn with large paddletail bird on plume decoration, very tight 6″ hairline in back, 17½″ tall, c. 1885. **$2400**

T. Harrington, Lyons, New York, six-gallon churn with starface decoration, professional restoration to overall glaze flaking in back and side, slight restoration in bottom of design, tight hairlines from churn use, and glaze flakes in front, 20″ tall, c. 1855. **$2000**

Unsigned five-gallon churn with floral wreath and date "1884," attributed to Fort Edward, New York, minor stone ping and spider line at rim, 17½" tall, c. 1884. **$1150**

Whites, Utica five-gallon churn with double bird decoration, good blue, professional restoration to very tight base line in back and a stone ping on rim done in the making, 18" tall, c. 1865. **$1850**

Co-operative Pottery Co., Lyons, New York, three-gallon churn, tight 6" line in front and 6" line in back also from use, 17" tall, c. 1900. **$180**

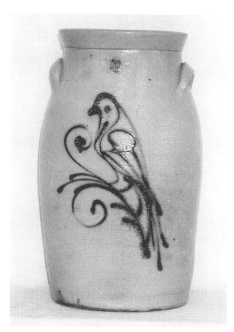

Unsigned four-gallon churn with large parrot on branch, attributed to Flack & Van Arsdale, Cornwell, Ontario, 16½" tall, c. 1880. **$300**

F. Stetzenmeyer & Co., Rochester, New York, four-gallon churn, full-length stabilized crack in back, 18" tall, c. 1855, original churn guide. **$8500**

Price Trends

To secure a deeper appreciation of where stoneware prices are going, it is worthwhile to briefly investigate where prices have been. The following pieces were advertised for sale between 1977 and 1981.

Selected Stoneware Prices from Garth's Auctions, 1977

Stoneware jug, blue transfer label, "Casey Bros., Scranton, PA." and "Pasteur Chamberland Filter Co., Dayton, Ohio," 7½". **$27.50**

Stoneware bottle, "Vimo, Ginger Beer, Cleveland, Ohio," 6½" high. **$11**

Stoneware flask, 8" high. **$37.50**

Six-gallon stoneware double-handled jar, signature in cobalt, "Lampert, Wenport," 19" high. **$37.50**

Stoneware jar, simple leaf in cobalt, 10¼" high. **$27.50**

Four-gallon butter crock, impressed signature, "A. O. Whittemore, Havana, N.Y.," well-drawn bird in cobalt. **$200**

85

Two-gallon jug, "J. and E. Norton, Bennington, Vt.," swirled cobalt design. **$135**

Two-gallon ovoid jug, "I. M. Mead," brushed cobalt flower. **$105**

Three-gallon stoneware jug, cobalt "3", 14½" high. **$17.50**

Miniature stoneware advertising jug, incised label, "Husch Bros., Louisville, Ky.," 3" high. **$14**

Four-gallon stoneware jar, stenciled label, "William and Reppert, Greensboro, Pa.," 14" high. **$27.50**

Six-gallon stoneware jug, cobalt label, "Grant and Colfax 1868," 16½" high. **$95**

Stoneware jar, stenciled cobalt label, "T. F. Reppert, Greensboro, Pa.," 9¾" high. **$32.50**

Stoneware jar, stenciled label, "Hamilton and Jones, Greensboro, Pa.," 8" high. **$45**

Redware plate, four-line yellow slip decoration with green, coggled edge, mint condition, 11½" diameter. **$375**

Redware pitcher, greenish tan glaze, 7¾" high. **$15**

Redware plate, yellow slip design with splashes of green, clear shiny glaze, 8" diameter. **$100**

Stoneware batter pitcher, Albany slip, worn painted flower, 7¾" high. **$2**

Stoneware jug, impressed signature, "N.Y. Stoneware Company," simple cobalt leaf design, 14" high. **$37.50**

Two-gallon stoneware batter pitcher, "E. Bishop, near Burlington, Ohio," blue brushed design at spout, 13½". **$75**

Three-gallon jar, "E. A. Montell, Olean, N.Y.," brushed cobalt flower, 10¾" high. **$65**

Three-gallon stoneware jar, "T. Reed," brushed cobalt tulip, 11½" high. **$195**

Stoneware canning jar, brushed cobalt designs, 9½" high. **$70**

Two-gallon batter pitcher, flower and squiggly lines, "1843" in cobalt slip, 13¾" high. **$280**

Ten-gallon stoneware crock, cobalt slip comic drawing of old woman with curly hair, 13½" diameter × 17¼" high. **$595**

Six-gallon stoneware crock, incised cow, cobalt "Gardiner Stone Ware, Manufactory, Gardiner, Me." **$55**

Three-gallon stoneware ovoid jug, cobalt brushed on at handle, 16¾" high. **$45**

Stoneware batter pitcher, brushed floral cobalt design. **$300**

Bennington covered jar, "1849" mark. **$265**

Stoneware "bird" crock, "New York Stoneware Co., North Edward, N.Y., 6," modern wooden lid, 8" high. **$105**

Five-gallon crock, three incised eagles, each with spear and banner, 12" high. **$85**

Stoneware butter crock, brushed blue feather designs, 8½" diameter. **$165**

Three-gallon crock, cobalt hen pecking corn, 10½" high. **$165**

Small wooden washboard, redware insert in wooden frame, 7" × 13½". **$37.50**

Stoneware jar, applied handles, brushed blue floral band, 13½" high. **$95**

Five-gallon stoneware jug, "Weading and Belding, Brantford, Ohio," brushed flower, 18½" high. **$65**

Three-gallon stoneware crock, gilt-work decoration, 13½" high. **$75**

Stoneware Advertised for Sale in 1980

Jugs

One-gallon, 10″ tall, "Wm. Radams Microbe Killer Co." **$30**

One-gallon, 10½″ tall, c. 1900, unsigned, molded, brown and white. **$12**

Three-gallon, 16″ tall, E. Norton, cobalt flower. **$130**

One-gallon, 11″ tall, signed "Haxstun Ottman," cobalt bird. **$165**

One-gallon, 12″ tall, Geddes, New York, cobalt decoration, "K. P. and Co." **$65**

One-gallon, 11½″ tall, N. White and Co., cobalt flying dove. **$335**

Two-gallon, 14″ tall, ovoid, c. 1820, unsigned, incised standing bird. **$1,500**

Two-gallon, 15″ tall, unsigned, ovoid, brushed tulip, base chip. **$150**

Three-gallon, 16″ tall, Jacob Caire, incised 8″ long detailed bird. **$1,100**

Two-gallon 13¼″ tall, W. A. Lewis, 6″ long cobalt bird. **$300**

Three-gallon, 14½″ tall, C. Hart, cobalt flower and stems. **$115**

One-gallon, 11″ tall, J. Norton, cobalt bird. **$325**

One-gallon, deep cobalt chicken pecking corn, Ballard and Scott, Cambridgeport, Massachusetts. **$395**

Three-gallon, 15½″ tall, West Troy, New York, large blue bird. **$170**

Two-gallon, 14½″ tall, Roberts, Binghamton, New York, great bird covering most of the front of the jug. **$295**

Two-gallon, ovoid, J. and C. Hart, Sherburne, New York, cobalt "2." **$135**

One-gallon, 11½″ tall, Whites' Utica, deep cobalt swirl "pine tree." **$75**

One-gallon, 11″ tall, Haxstun and Company, Fort Edward, New York, simple cobalt flower. **$65**

One-half-gallon, 9″ tall, c. 1900, unsigned, no decoration, cream-colored body. **$9**

Two-gallon, 14¼″ tall, Whites' Utica, deep cobalt "flamingo" looking over its shoulder. **$225**

Crocks

One-and-one-half-gallon, 8½″ tall, cobalt fern. **$70**

Two-gallon, 9½″ tall, unsigned, cobalt bird on a branch. **$160**

Six-gallon, 13″ tall, N. A. White and Son, Utica, New York, large deep cobalt orchid. **$225**

Four-gallon, 12″ tall, West Troy, New York, simple bird on a branch. **$175**

Three-gallon, 10″ tall, unsigned, rim chips, deep cobalt bird. **$160**

Four-gallon, 11″ tall, E. Norton and Co., large cobalt flower. **$135**

One-and-one-half-gallon, 8½″ tall, Brady and Ryan, blue bird on a branch. **$150**

Three-gallon, 10″ tall, unsigned, cobalt sketch of profile of a man in uniform. **$550**

Two-gallon, 9½″ tall, Burger and Lang, deep cobalt flower. **$165**

Three-gallon, 10½″ tall, New York Stoneware Co., deep cobalt great spread-winged bird landing on a stump. **$800**

Two-gallon, 9½″ tall, unsigned, fat bird on a branch. **$185**

Two-gallon, 9½″ tall, S. Hart, two birds on a branch. **$185**

Three-gallon, 10½" tall, Brady and Ryan, Ellenville, New York, cobalt chicken pecking corn. **$255**

Two-gallon, 9" tall, unsigned, deep cobalt bird on a log. **$175**

Two-gallon, 8½" tall, J. Burger, Rochester, New York, two feathers with a cobalt swirl inside. **$145**

Two-gallon, 9½" tall, Haxstun and Company, Ft. Edward, New York, fat bird on a branch. **$175**

Pitchers

Six-quart, 11" tall, unsigned, cobalt bird, repaired crack. **$250**

One-gallon, 10" tall, unsigned, simple cobalt bird on a branch. **$775**

One-gallon, 11" tall, signed J. Burger, geometric cobalt design and "1." **$335**

One-and-one-half gallon, West Troy, New York, large cobalt feather. **$395**

One-gallon, 11½" tall, Lyons, New York, deep cobalt bird on a branch. **$775**

Miscellaneous stoneware

Lodge hall spittoon, "I.O.O.F. No. 15," unsigned, 5½" diameter. **$185**

Two-gallon covered jar, 11" tall, W. H. Farrar/Geddes, New York, deep cobalt flowers and stems, ovoid. **$245**

Batter pail, one-gallon, 9¼" tall, unsigned, no lid. **$33**

Churn, three-gallon, 14" tall, E. S. Fox, Athens, New York, ovoid, double cobalt flower. **$295**

Ovoid jar, one-gallon, 11" tall, Warner, West Troy, New York, cobalt swirl. **$100**

Butter crock, three- to four-gallon, 7¼" tall, unsigned, original lid, cobalt flowers and vines. **$395**

Blue-painted knife and fork box. $200

Cyclone wheelbarrow. $300

Blown jars with paper labels. $125 each

Tin spice chest. $385

Blown-glass jar with original mohair contents. $250

New England wash basket. $175

Child's Harvard farm wagon. $1500

Painted four-drawer spice chest. $225

Child's watering can. $85

Sponge-decorated pitcher. $250

Schoenhut clown ($150) and brown bear ($450)

Two-gallon Pennsylvania jar. $200

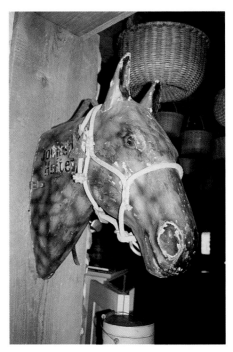

*Lodge hall papier-mâché skeleton and wood-
en casket.* **$500**

Salesman's suitcase for horse halters. **$400**

Counter desk with grained paint. **$285**

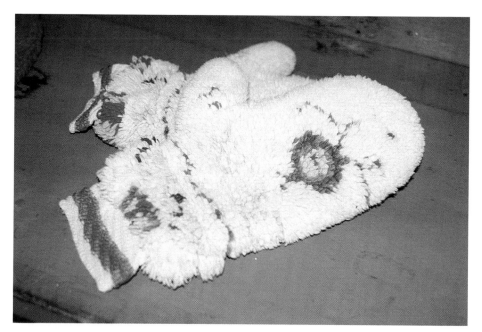

Hooked mittens. $225

Feather tree with turned base. $335

Straw-filled Santa Claus, 1930s. $345

Bamby Bread broom holder. $215

TYPE & SIZE	MARK OR POTTER	DESCRIPTION

UNUSUAL FORM

TYPE & SIZE	MARK OR POTTER	DESCRIPTION
Chick waterer 1 pint 5½" tall	(NONE) (c1850–c1875)	Blue topped finial, ½" wide blue stripe over joint of jug form and cupped opening. Blue around lip of opening. Rare miniature. Slight chipping on lip. **$135**
Milk pan 1½ gal. 12½" wide 4¾" tall	(NONE) (Penn., c1875)	Impressed "1½" in circle. Pour spout and two handles. Six blue floral designs encircling, blue at handles. Repaired lip chip. Two tight hairlines. **$105**

EARLY STONEWARE

TYPE & SIZE	MARK OR POTTER	DESCRIPTION
Ovoid jug 1 gal. 12" tall	J. Remmey Manhattan-Wells New York (c1800–c1810)	Bright blue in mark and at handles, deep gray clay. John Remmey, III, a very rare mark. Two tiny chips at base, small pebble-burst chip near base. Nice ringed neck. **$425**
Ovoid pot with fine vertical loop handles, about 1½ gal. 11¾" tall	(NONE) (possibly early Remmey New York c1775–c1800)	Deeply incised fleur-de-lis design (7¾") on both sides, filled in brilliant blue. Two very minor hairlines at base. Tight base separation probably filled by potter (appears as nearly invisible line around foot of pot). **$350**
Snuff jar ½ gal. 8" tall	(NONE) (attributed to Old Bridge, NJ, area c1820)	Impressed design (completely encircling the piece at collar) of alternating fish and four "cherries," six fish and bunches of cherries in all (each fish 1⅝"). Shiny dark blue over entire design. Perfect. **$350**
Ovoid pot with two horizontal, nearly free-standing handles close to collar 2 gal. 11½" tall	(NONE) (attributed to Frederick Carpenter of Charlestown and Boston, c1801–c1810)	Impressed ribbed swag between two tassels (design on front and back) filled in rich blue. Couple of very minor lip chips. Very bulbous pot. **$275**

TYPE & SIZE	MARK OR POTTER	DESCRIPTION
Ovoid jug 1 quart 8⅝" tall	(NONE) (probably Hartford, CT, c1815–c1830)	Beautiful neck with 5 tooled rings. Shiny brown slip overall. Nice slender ovoid form. Very minor base chips. **$35**
Jug 1 pint 6⅝" tall	(NONE) (c1850–c1875)	Partially curved sides, varied tan slip. Tiny chip on side of handle. Potter's finger marks at base. **$15**

NORTON OF BENNINGTON, VT

TYPE & SIZE	MARK OR POTTER	DESCRIPTION
Crock 1 gal. 7¼" tall	E & L P Norton Bennington, VT (1861–1881)	Bright blue typical oak leaf filled in blue. Cute size. Perfect. **$110**
Crock 3 gal. 10¼" tall	E & L P Norton Bennington, VT (1861–1881)	Bird (7¼") with teardrop wing on leaf. Good blue, some minor blurring due to heavy salt glaze. Very nearly perfect. **$250**
Ovoid jug 1 gal. 10½" tall	L. Norton & Son (1833–1838)	Two leaves with trailing squiggle (almost a moth). Medium blue. Small spot of light brown slip to left of mark. Very nearly perfect. **$245**
Snuff jar 1 gal. 8¾" tall	L. Norton & Son (1833–1838)	Very rare Bennington form. Covered with deep brown, shiny slip. Slight hairline, minor tiny rim chip. **$60**
Low butter crock 1 gal. 5" tall	E. Norton & Co. Bennington, VT (1881–c1885)	Rare form, some blue in mark. No handles. Perfect. **$50**
Crock 1 gal. 7" tall	L. Norton & Son (1833–1838)	Covered with brown, tan, reddish brown slip. Nice coloring effect. Rare for straight-sided crock of such an early date. Very nearly perfect. **$60**
Semi-ovoid pot 1 gal. 9" tall	E & L P Norton Bennington, VT (1861–1881)	Large ornate blue leaf. Unusual slender tall crock with small handles. "Bennington" in mark is very faint. Good salt glaze. Three tight hairlines, one in front (very tight, not in design), two small ones in back, all 2"–3" down from top. **$95**

TYPE & SIZE	MARK OR POTTER	DESCRIPTION
DECORATION		
Crock 2 gal. 9″ tall	Edmands & Co. Charlestown, Mass. c1850–c1865	Large bird (8″) full of dots, sitting on foliage. Great blue. Two-inch chip out of back rim. Couple of minor rim chips. **$185**
Cream pot 2 gal. 12½″ tall	(NONE)	Unusual bird with speckled breast on flowered branch. Some water glass inside, small tight hairline. Nice blue on gray clay. **$150**

CHAPTER SEVEN

Kitchen and Hearth Antiques

This chapter was prepared by Teri and Joe Dziadul. It illustrates items from their personal collection. The Dziaduls have been filling special requests for more than 20 years and offer kitchen and hearth antiques for sale to collectors and dealers. The current list of items for sale may be obtained by sending $1 to the Dziaduls at:

6 South George Washington Road
Enfield, CT 06082

Colonial Kitchen Gadgets

In colonial New England, the snow often lay half-a-yard deep near the Connecticut River and a yard deep about the Merrimack. With snowflakes as great as shillings and tempests of wind and snow, the warming hearth was the center of the house. The raging fury of the storms thundered down the chimneys; and, in the morning, frost crystals could be seen on the chimney back over the raked-up fire. Interior temperatures were remarkably cold. China cups on the tea table cracked from the frost the instant hot tea touched them. In cold north bedchambers, where the sun never shone, snow sifted in through window cracks and ice and frost reigned with supremacy to create a great storehouse repository of frozen-solid surplus treasures. Pies baked at Thanksgiving often came out fresh and good with the violets of April. Cranberries kept well in water and if frozen, so much the better. Strings of dried apples, peppers, and pumpkins looped in gay festoons across the room along with dried bouquets of sage, savory, mint, thyme, and other herbs. Crookneck squashes hung in racks set against the wall.

Triple foot warmer, accommodates three pairs of feet, 21½" long, c. 1820, fitted with iron or tin pan of glowing coals for warmth in pew or parlor. (Margaret Bayard Smith wrote in her book A Winter in Washington on 19 January 1871, "Half frozen, with my back close to the fire and a foot stove beneath my feet." These were considered a feminine amenity.) **$775–$875**

Double foot warmer, tin, wooden frame, original tin warming pan, 16", c. 1840. **$550–$650**

Round and oval foot warmers, scarcer than single square foot stoves. **$450–$550**

Left: *Tin ale warmer with collapsible handle,* **$250–$295.** Center: *Warmer with wood handle and pewter knob,* **$350–$395.** Right: *Covered ale shoe with copper toe,* **$650–$850** (*These hearth accessories had hot coals heaped around them and ale shoes were thrust directly into hot coals.*)

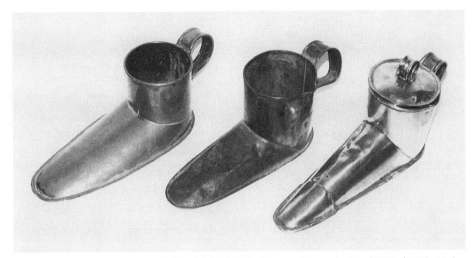

Copper ale shoes. Left: *Broad ale shoe,* **$550–$650.** Center: *Short ale shoe,* **$575–$675.** Right: *Covered ale shoe,* **$750–$850.**

Cast-iron patented stove and lantern with ornate design in casting, round lid marked "F. Arnold's Combined Stove & Lantern— Patent Applied for 1853. Manufactured at Middle Haddam, CT." **$425–$495**

Candle-related items. Left: *Large wood candle box, stenciled on side "I. Allen—Blackrock 45 lbs. Candles," rosehead-type nails,* **$227–$275;** Left and right: *Three- and four-tube tin candle molds, scalloped base,* **$190–$290;** Rear: *Tin tallow skimmer, exceptionally long wood handle,* **$425–$475;** *tallow candles,* **$65–$95** *each; framed wood candle mold with 24 pewter tubes,* **$995–$1100;** Right front: *Framed candle mold with 12 redware tubes, each tube marked "A Wilcox," a New York State maker, wire rods across top hold wicks in place above each opening,* **$1400–$1500.**

Caroline King, author of *When I Lived in Salem,* recounts that tall conical-shaped pyramids of loaf sugar stood in a row like a party of masqueraders, cloaked in long purple and blue dominoes. Their bright labels fastened with little bows of red ribbon formed gay aprons. Sugar nippers broke up these cones so they could be pulverized in lignum vitae mortars. Once pulverized, sugar was often kept in treen sugar bowls now known as Peaseware. Peaseware is named for Hiram Pease, who erected a sawmill in Ohio around 1840 for turning, planing, and joining

wood. The area he worked in has since become known as Pease Hollow. It was there that he turned on his lathes the pieces we value as heirlooms today. Susanna Whaleman's mid-eighteenth-century manuscript housekeeping book outlined for her servants' benefit her wishes for breaking and storing sugar: "Plenty of sugar should always be kept ready broke in the deep sugar drawers in the closet storeroom. There is one for spice, one for moist sugar, and two for lump sugar. The pieces should be as square as possible, and rather small. The sugar that is powdered to fill the sugar castor should be kept in a basin in one of the drawers to prevent any insects getting into it and be powdered fine in the mortar and kept ready for use."

The day was never long enough for the housewife who often had to feed a family of ten or more. Endless preparation was required before actual cooking could begin—cutting, shredding, chopping, beating, grinding, mixing, pitting, and paring. As timesaving devices were invented, each new gadget that could afford relief to the cook was welcomed with much enthusiasm. Apple parers were extremely useful since apples were a household staple for pies, sauce, apple butter, and cider. At harvest time, a single household might have pared three hundred bushels of apples for use in the winter months. Through an arrangement of gears that operated revolving wire beaters, the egg beater accelerated the manual beating process. Thousands of patents were issued for household devices. Some were cumbersome in their construction, but

many were simple and forthright, possessing an inherent beauty through honest lines and forms. In Victorian times, manufacturers began to decorate these appliances with elaborate designs to disguise their utilitarian purpose, preferring to create objects which were believed to be aesthetic additions to the home.

There is scant record of the use and design of butter molds. They are the product of artisans who were familiar with birds, animals, plants, and fruit. Their art experience was limited, but their design sense was great. In the marketplace, the butter producer was identified by his design which took on a trademark value. Like butter molds, candle molds have a rather unsophisticated, utilitarian charm. They required a knot to be tied at the small end of the mold to keep the hot tallow wax from running out. With the refinement of the pewter tips, the problem of hole enlarging was eliminated. A tin strap was soldered at the top to keep tubes from moving and a hinged holder secured

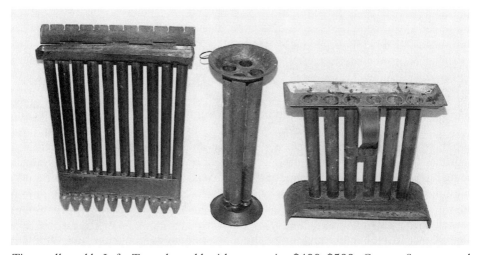

Tin candle molds. Left: *Ten-tube mold with pewter tips,* **$400–$500.** Center: *Scarce round four-tube mold,* **$350–$400.** Right: *Six-tube mold with stretcher base,* **$350–$400.**

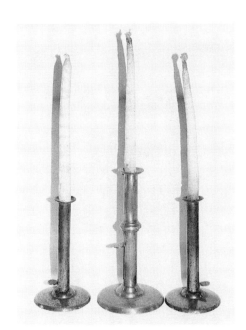

Steel hog-scraper candlesticks (they derive their name from a similarity to a device, and their occasional use as such, for scraping hog bristles at butchering time). Left and right: *Signed pair,* **$375–$475.** Center: *9½" tall, marked "Dowler," c. 1751–1808, steel ring around shaft,* **$675–$775.** *Tallow candles,* **$65–$95** each

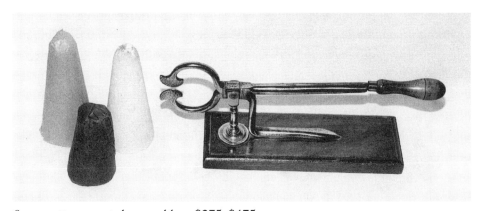

Sugar cutters mounted on wood base. **$375–$475**

the wick over each opening. Samuel H. Bingham (1854–1906), a Pennsylvania tinsmith, indicated in his account books that he made many candle molds, some at 62½ cents each and some at 87½ cents each.

Colonial kitchen utensils were fashioned from wood, stoneware, pewter, tin, iron, copper, and brass. The market value of kitchen and hearth antiques often rises and falls according to current popularity. Rare examples of patented gadgets remain at consistently high price levels. Acquiring kitchen antiques can be an art. However, it requires knowledge, skill, and patience. For most of us, it is a consuming interest that is fun and can last a lifetime.

Iron boot scraper with weighted base. **$175–$275**

Make-do's (broken objects ingeniously repaired with tin handles, bases, etc.) now comprise a much-desired collecting category. Goblets, **$125–$175.** *Sandwich glass whale-oil lamp,* **$225–$275.**

Peaseware treen sugar bowls: Medium-size bowl, **$675–$875;** *large bowl,* **$2200–$2600;** *small bowl,* **$325–$375.**

Peaseware treen pieces: small sugar bowl, **$325–$395;** *medium jar, sometimes referred to as "lighthouse form," for storage of herbs or spices,* **$400–$500;** *spool holder with hole for thread to be pulled out as needed,* **$350–$395.**

Wood breadboard, referred to as the "wedding board," a scarce example. **$300–$375**

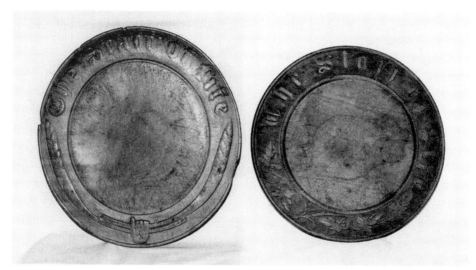

Wood breadboards. Left: *Unusual carving with hand holding wheat heads,* **$175–$200.** Right: *Remarkable carving of leaves and letters,* **$250–$295.**

Treen plates, 1790–1820, light weight and "ovaling" out are good indicators of age.
$225–$325 *each*

Left and right: *Treen plates, c. 1800,* **$225–$300.** Center: *Treen deep dish, c. 1800,*
$300–$375.

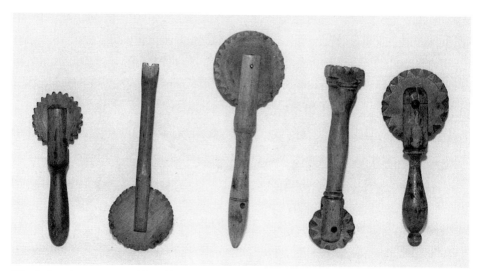

Wood pie crimpers, turned handles, two with imprints on ends for marking dough. $75–$150 each

Wood lemon reamers, $145–$250 *(with folded tin sections in head,* $175–$195*)*

Carved wood Indian eating spoons.
$85–$145

Painted pantry boxes. Left: *Mustard yellow bottom, black lid,* **$375–$475.** Right: *Dark green paint,* **$400–$475.**

Eleven-drawer spice cabinet, 23" high, the tea and coffee drawers are very unusual. $375–$475

Wood spice chests with pewter scroll labels (left), **$275–$350;** *with porcelain rosette knobs* (right), **$300–$375.**

106

Wood spice chests, stenciled labels on drawers. **$325–$395**

Wood rolling pins. Left: *Framed with double supports,* **$350–$400.** Right: *Very scarce example for kneading dough,* **$250–$295.**

Ornamental treen sugar mold and springerle molds. Left and right: *Alpine men springerle blocks,* **$100–$150.** Center: *Sugar mold with biblical symbols from* Genesis IX, **$350–$395.**

Animal and bird butter stamps and butter mold. Top row, left to right: *Half-round stamp, eagle carving,* **$875–$975;** *sheep mold,* **$600–$700;** *half-round stamp, cow carving, very scarce motif,* **$1000–$1200.** Bottom row, left to right: *Squirrel stamp,* **$875–$975;** *eagle stamp,* **$475–$575;** *running fox stamp,* **$900–$1000.**

Various butter stamps and molds. Top row, left to right: *Elliptical stamp with geometric carving,* **$475–$575;** *square box mold, excellent condition (many of these block cake molds are cracked and in poor condition),* **$275–$300;** *round double-sided stamp with geometric carving,* **$475–$575.** Bottom row, left to right: *Oblong stamp, carved Christmas and holly leaves and berries,* **$667–$775;** *half-round stamp, pineapple carving,* **$600–$700.**

Fruits and berries butter stamps and butter mold. Top row, left to right: *Triple strawberry,* **$275–$300;** *carved apple mold,* **$225–$275;** *pear,* **$195–$250.** Bottom row, left to right: *Apple stamp,* **$125–$150;** *double strawberry stamp,* **$150–$200;** *gooseberries stamp, difficult design to locate,* **$275–$300.**

Cylinder butter stamps with pewter bands (case and insert design must have matching numbers, otherwise they are not original to each other). Left to right: *One-pound, thistle,* **$225–$275;** *two-pound, strawberry,* **$300–$350;** *one-pound, pineapple,* **$225–$275.**

Soft-paste butter stamps. Left to right: *Grapes,* **$600–$675;** *large ear of corn,* **$750–$800;** *small ear of corn,* **$600–$675.**

Higgins shop basket, very sturdy (used in mills and other places of manufacture). **$400–$500**

Three-piece butter mold, double eagle print (noted in old catalog as a Seely mold but location unknown). **$400–$500**

Higgins baskets. Small, fixed handle, **$400–$475;** *pie basket, paper label reads "Guaranteed Pounded Ash—Manufactured by B. G. Higgins—West Chesterfield, MA.,"* **$425–$475.**

Higgins bushel basket, scarce size.
$400–$500

Higgins knitting basket, unusual form.
$300–$400

Higgins covered basket, rare. **$400–$500**

Covered pie basket, wide splint, elevated inner pie rack. **$75–$95**

Multi-purpose tin tools (often referred to as the Kitchen Magician, patented by Sydney Cooke of Bayonne City, New Jersey, April 26, 1870) perform several functions: Dredger, doughnut cutter on inside of lid, cookie cutter on bottom, one grating surface for nutmeg, the other for lemon peel, and jagging wheel, scarce and difficult to find intact. **$1000–$1500** *each*

Telephone coffee mill, hardwood back, fancy cast-iron front, c. 1890. **$225–$300**

Flour sifter, tin and cast iron, c. 1890. **$225–$300**

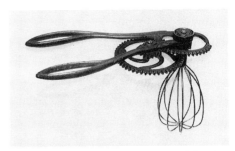

Jaquette Bros. #3 beater, patented in four sizes by Harry Jaquette of Philadelphia. **$650–$750**

Meat and vegetable chopper (also referred to as a steamboat chopper, patented 1865 by Leroy Starrett, Athol Depot, Massachusetts). **$250–$350**

Silver's trademark Brooklyn eggbeater, bridge embossed on jar bottom (listed in 1918 Sears catalog for $1.45). **$225–$275**

E-Z mixer, patented by Luther E. Shinn, Pittsburgh, 1902. **$450–$500**

Keystone wall-mount beater (left), *December 15, 1885,* **$275–$300.** *Holt's eggbeater* (right), *patented 1899, jar embossed "Sanety wide mouth Mason-Salem Glass Works, Salem, NJ,"* **$350–$450.**

Child's beater, Delta, Detroit decal, 5" high. **$75–$85**

Rumford tin items. Left to right: *Biscuit cutter,* **$12–$18;** *measuring cup,* **$20–$30;** *dough-nut cutter,* **$14–$20.**

Tin ring mold (another food color can be pressed in tips at top). $110–$125

Tin Liberty-embossed ABC plate. $125–$175

Tin peanut butter pails: Sultana, $75–$95; Long's Ox-Heart brand, $110–$125.

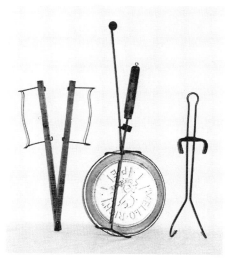

Wire utensils. Left to right: *Tenderizer, 6½″ high,* **$50–$75;** *double-grid potato masher,* **$65–$85;** *spiral wire eggbeater,* **$16–$20;** *miniature wire basket,* **$95–$125.**

Pie lifters, wire and iron, **$28–$75.** *Tin pie plate* (center), **$12–$18.**

Terra-cotta apple, **$125–$175.** *Plaster loaf of bread,* **$45–$55.**

Chocolate molds. Left to right: *Father Christmas,* **$125–$150;** *St. Nicholas (Bishop of Myra),* **$350–$400;** *Belsnickel,* **$150–$175.**

Chocolate molds: 20-inch Belsnickel, **$4000–$4500;** *7-inch Belsnickel with switches,* **$300–$350.**

118

Chocolate molds: 17-inch rabbit, $300–$350; 12-inch rabbit, $275–$300.

Miniature treen pieces. Clockwise from top: *Castor set,* **$150–$175;** *piggen,* **$250–$300;** *jug with iron nail handle,* **$75–$85;** *three-legged kettle,* **$125–$175;** *pail, signed "Wm. S. BOWER, So. Hingham, Mass.,"* **$425–$475;** *salt box,* **$225–$275;** *mortar and pestle,* **$75–$85.**

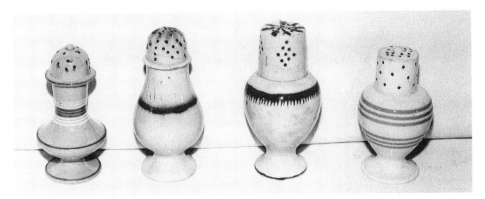

Pepper pots. Left to right: *Mocha, blue and cream banding,* $225–$275; *Leeds, green feathering,* $125–$150; *Leeds, blue decoration,* $175–$200; *white, blue banding,* $125–$150.

Pepper pots. Left to right: *Pink transfer ware,* $175–$195; *mocha, blue with black bands,* $325–$375; *blue willow,* $150–$200; *pink lustre,* $125–$150.

Mustard pots. Left to right: *Leeds, green feathering,* $175–$200; *Leeds, blue feathering,* $200–$225; *mocha, black and brown,* $345–$375.

Blue onion dinner plates and soup bowl, marked "Meissen." **$65–$85** *each*

Blue onion compotes, marked "Meissen." **$175–$200** *each*

Staffordshire plate and teapot: Blue plate marked "Clews Warranted, Staffordshire Peace and Plenty," **$275–$325;** *brown transfer teapot, marked "Franklin's Moral Pictures," some chips, needs bleaching,* **$200–$250.**

Blue spongeware bowl. **$250–$300**

Cake stands. $75–$95 *each*

Blown glass storage jars. Left to right: *Teardrop knob on lid, attributed to Sandwich, applied sapphire blue rings,* **$475–$575;** *mushroom finial on lid, applied clear crimped rings,* **$145–$175;** *large mushroom knob on lid, applied sapphire blue rings,* **$575–$675.**

Candy jars. Left to right: *Small bulbous jar, ground stopper,* **$175–$195;** *medium bulbous jar, ground stopper,* **$200–$250;** *teardrop knob, swirl,* **$200–$250.**

Candy jars, 13¼" high, 2" diameter, ground stoppers, swirl design. **$225–$250** *pair*

Ice-cream-related items. Left to right, back to front; row 1: *Jiffy Dispenser Co. dipper, patented 1925, curved to fit side of container used for ice cream sandwiches,* **$350–$400;** *Dover Mfg. Co. springless dipper, c. 1929,* **$150–$195;** *copper and chrome ice cream soda shop display,* **$800–$900;** *Gilchrist cone-shaped dipper, No. 33,* **$150–$175;** *Clipper dipper, F.S. Co., Troy, New York,* **$200–$225;** row 2: *rectangular tin ice cream sandwich wafer holder,* **$85–$95;** *round tin ice cream sandwich wafer holder, rare,* **$200–$225;** row 3: *penny and tuppenny ice cream licks,* **$50–$75** *each;* row 4: *Quick and Easy cone-shaped dipper, Erie Specialty Co., Erie, Pennsylvania,* **$225–$250;** *General ice cream disher,* **$1100–$1200.**

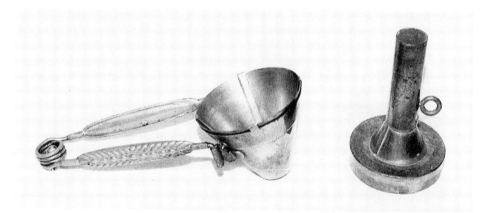

Ice-cream-related items: Kingery ice cream disher, c. 1892, bowl rotates when handle is squeezed, **$300–$375;** *round tin ice cream sandwich wafer holder,* **$200–$225.**

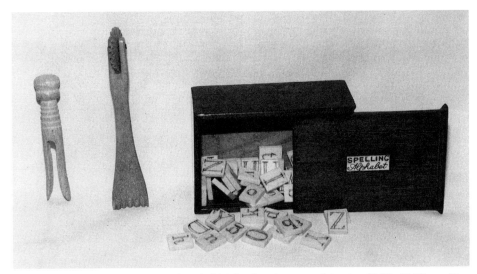

Bone items: whalebone clothespin, $225–$295; pie crimper and jagger, $150–$175; spelling alphabet letters in box, whalebone letters, box with bone inset in lid, two sets of letters, $250–$300.

Brass rag picker's bell. $275–$300

Architectural units: gilt acorn, **$125–$150;** *iron acorn from gatepost,* **$75–$95;** *artichoke, blue-green paint, poor base,* **$85–$95.**

Original watercolor by Tasha Tudor, from 1993 edition of Tasha Tudor Cookbook. **$8000–$9000**

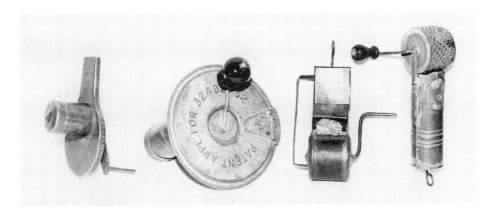

Mechanical nutmeg graters. Left to right: *Tin bellows grater,* **$600–$675;** *tin, late 19th century,* **$750–$850;** *all tin, patented November 1855,* **$675–$725;** *tin and wood, impressed "M. H. Sexton, Utica, NY, Pat'd May 1896,"* **$900–$1000.**

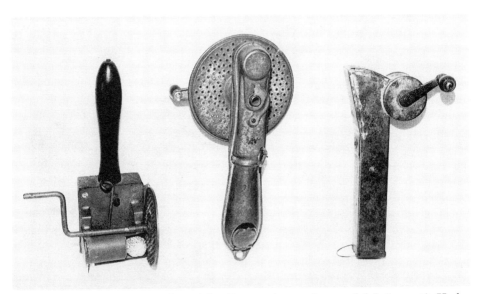

Mechanical nutmeg graters. Left to right: *Rotary, tin, wood, paper label, Brown & Hasler, Lynn, Massachusetts,* **$900–$1000;** *tin, handle has storage for nutmegs,* **$900–$1000;** *tin, marked "Davidson Automatic Nutmeg Grater,"* **$800–$1000.**

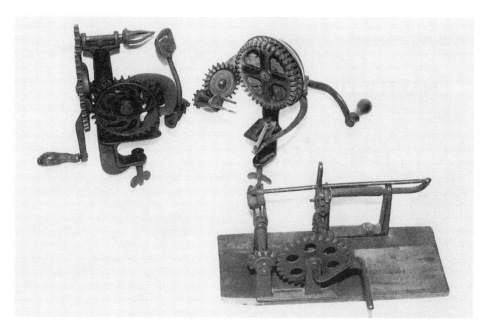

Apple parers. Top left: *"The Union Mf'd by D. H. Whittemore, Worcester, Mass. Pat. Nov. 11, 1866,"* **$300–$350;** Top right: *"F. L. Hudson's Improved, Leonminster, Mass. Pat. Dec. 2, 1862,"* **$275–$325;** Bottom: *"Larned & Seagraves, Worcester, Mass.,"* mounted on board, geared to transfer three rotations of fork with each crank rotation, c. 1855, **$175–$200.**

Highly complex apple parer, The Climax, marked "Geo. W. Brokaw, Lodi, N.Y., Pat. May 11, 1869." This is the ultimate collector's goal. Once the paring operation is complete, a separate set of gears engage, indexing the apple and chopping slices from it. It resets to the original gears in readiness for the next apple. Without a doubt, this is ingenuity at its highest level. There is limited market experience for this parer, therefore a wide price range is given. **$1000–$1500**

CHAPTER EIGHT

Coffee Mills

Dr. Joseph MacMillan, author of *The MacMillan Index of Antique Coffee Mills,* provided the text and illustrations for this chapter. Dr. MacMillan's book is the definitive text on antique coffee mills. The heavily illustrated book contains more than 1,300 pages of information about coffee mills and the individuals and factories that produced them. It is available from Dr. MacMillan for $94 (postpaid). Write to him at:

657 Old Mountain Road
Marietta, GA 30064-1339

While antique coffee mills are not that difficult to find, their original source and value usually remain unknown to admirers and collectors. When one hears that the Peugeot Automobile Co. in France first made coffee mills and also that IBM manufactured coffee mills long before they built computers, it is obvious that there is more to the subject than one might at first believe. No collector's item has ever been made by so many and in such diverse shapes and types.

With interest in coffee in general sweeping the nation, the collecting of such delightful antiques will undoubtedly increase dramatically. The following illustrations of lap, wall, table, floor, and electric mills will give you an idea of the prices and sources of the coffee mills often seen in antiques malls and shops.

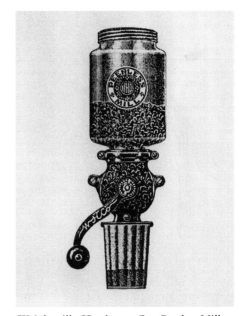

Wrightsville Hardware Co., Peerless Mill, c. 1915. **$300**

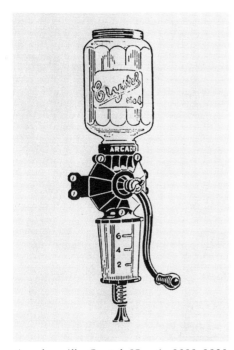

Arcade mill, Crystal No. 4, 1898–1930. **$300–$400**

Belmont Hardware Co. wall mills, c. 1907. **$150–$200** *each*

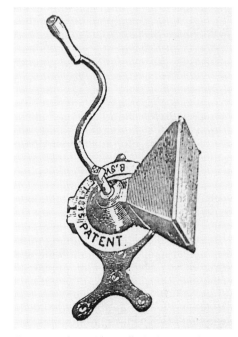

Lane Brothers side mill, Swift, 1845–1922. **$100–$175**

Bronson & Walton mill, Silver Lake, 1905–1915. **$275–$325**

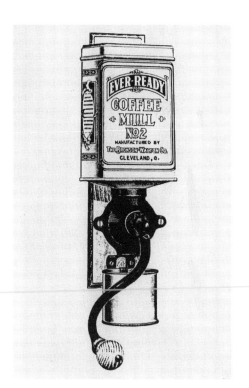

Enterprise cast-iron wall mill, c. 1889. **$350–$400**

Bronson & Walton mill, No. 2 Ever-Ready, c. 1909. **$200**

Enterprise wall mill with original receiver, No. 100, c. 1917. **$300**

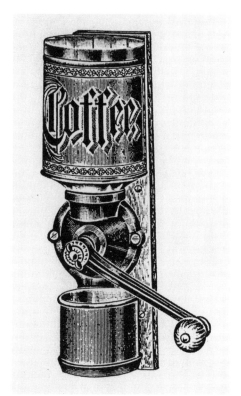

Arcade wall mill, "Coffee," c. 1900. **$150–$225**

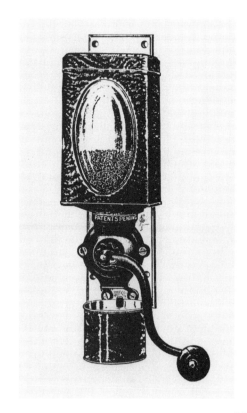

Bronson & Walton mill, mahogany, c. 1910. **$200–$275**

National Coffee Roasting Association mill, c. 1922. **$250–$350**

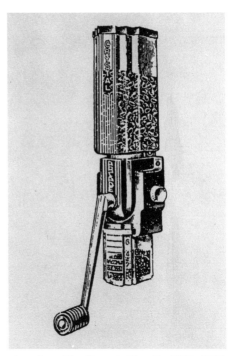

Arcade mill, Crystal No. 3, 1898–1930. **$275–$325**

Arcade Art Deco mill, No. 9010, 1920s. **$300–$400**

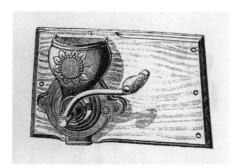

Waddell side mill, No. A-17, c. 1902.
$150–$250

Waddell lap mill, 1889–1892. **$230–$275**

Arcade mill, No. 777, c. 1900. **$350–$450**

Arcade "Telephone Mill," No. 1, early 1900s.
$900–$1500

Cavanaugh Bros. mill, c. 1886. **$200–$250**

Norton Bros. canister mill, c. 1887.
$325–$375

Logan & Strowbridge mill, 1876–1904.
$175–$250

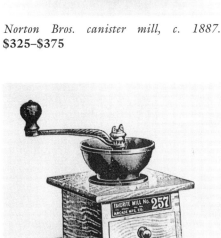

Arcade mill, No. 257, c. 1900. **$125–$175**

LaLance & Grosjean mill, No. 65, c. 1890.
$175–$200

Toy coffee mills, late 1880s–1930s. **$80–$90**

Universal lap mill, 1890–1910. **$175**

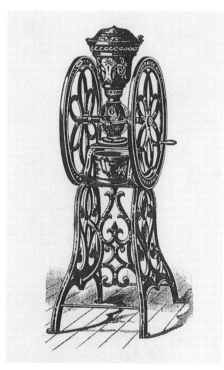

Enterprise floor mill, 1873–1910. **$1800–$3500**

Landers, Frary & Clark floor mill, 1910–1919. **$1300–$1800**

Enterprise Champion mill, No. 1, 1870–1880. **$1800–$3000**

Enterprise mill, No. 2, 1873–1920. **$500–$1000**

Coles counter mill, 1891–1910. **$600–$750**

Woodruff & Edwards floor mill, 1890–1910. **$1000–$1400**

CHAPTER NINE

Where to Buy

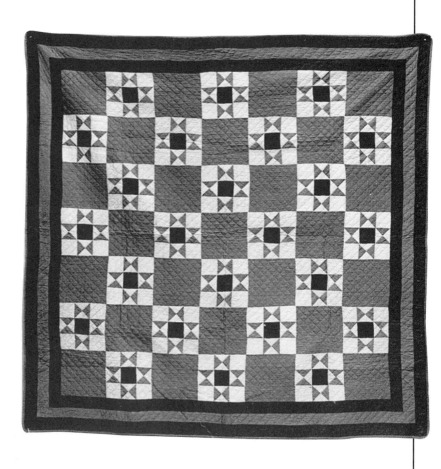

Shops, Auctions, and Markets

American Roots

American Roots is a group shop that specializes in Americana and country antiques. The shop is located in historic Old Towne Orange near the traffic circle at 105 Chapman Avenue in Orange, California. The shop hours are Tuesday through Saturday from 10 A.M. to 5 P.M. and on Sundays from noon to 5 P.M.

The nine experienced dealers who operate the shop stock painted furniture, vintage textiles, stoneware, toys, and architectural pieces. American Roots may be reached by telephone at (714) 639-3424.

Bakery sign, oyster white background and black lettering. **$165**

Top: *School bus sign, yellow background and black lettering, 1930s,* **$225.** Bottom: *Oval game board, New England, nineteenth century, brown and white with stenciled edge,* **$495.**

Back: *Set of drawers, apple green paint, c. 1900,* **$295.** Front: *Early knife-and-fork box, red paint with heart cutout on handle,* **$145.**

Wardrobe, pine, old paint, found in rural Ohio, c. 1900. **$1695**

Back: *Field basket, early white paint,* **$225.**
Front: *Indian baskets* (left to right): **$175,**
$165, $185.

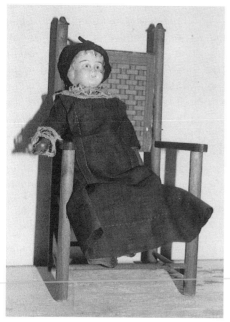

Stack of painted firkins (bottom to top):
Blue, **$295;** *blue-gray,* **$225;** *red,* **$195.**

Early "tin head" doll, original clothing.
$175

Valentine hooked rug, early 1900s. **$295**

Mustard painted hanging wall cupboard, pine, nineteenth century. $650

Pine apothecary cabinet, brown-red stain. $750

Shaker pie basket, blue-gray paint. **$295**

Star quilt, excellent condition, mustard, blue, and brown. **$295**

Rocking chair, strong red paint, black and mustard stenciled decoration. **$145**

Red marshmallow tin, early 1900s. **$195**

Tin heart-shaped cake molds, nest of four. **$245**

Penny rug, diamond-shaped, wool, excellent original condition. **$110**

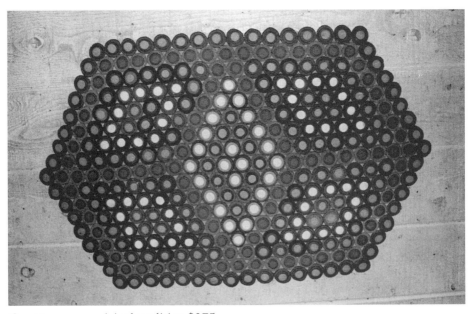

Great penny rug, original condition. **$275**

Large dollhouse, c. 1920, red and white paint. **$395**

Eight-drawer chest, apple green paint, originally for spices. **$275**

Teddy bears (left to right): *Straw-filled American bear, brown mohair, 1930s,* **$285;** *straw-filled bear, gold mohair, glass eyes, 1930s,* **$485;** *kapok-filled bear, probably American in origin, mohair, 1910–1930,* **$325;** *straw-filled American bear, button eyes, c. 1920s,* **$250.**

Asahel Gridley Antiques

Asahel Gridley Antiques is a large general-line shop in downtown Bloomington, Illinois, that is reminiscent of the antiques emporiums of 30 years ago. The shop carries a significant collection of walnut and pine furniture with an emphasis on nineteenth-century cupboards. The shop is open Wednesday–Saturday from 11 A.M. until 5 P.M.

Additional information can be secured by contacting:

Asahel Gridley Antiques
217–219 East Front Street
Bloomington, IL 61702
Telephone: (309) 829-9615

Nickel-plated copper teakettle, early 1900s. **$40**

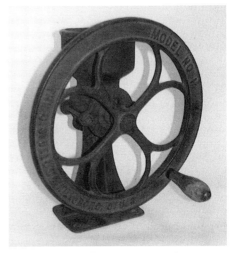

Early twentieth-century cast-iron corn grinder, painted red. **$85**

Two-gallon midwestern crock, stenciled "2" capacity mark, c. 1900. **$45**

Oak splint utility basket, 9" diameter. **$65**

Cardboard boxes of "Big John Plug Cut" tobacco, c. 1915. $6 each

Unused "Old Home Town" cigar cuttings for chewing and smoking, 1920s. $8

Child's tricycle, 1940s, original condition. $100

Galvanized watering can, 1930s–1940s. $20

Unused coffee bags, 1940s. $5 each

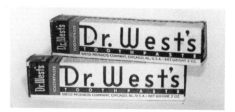

Unused Dr. West's toothpaste boxes, c. 1940. $6 each

149

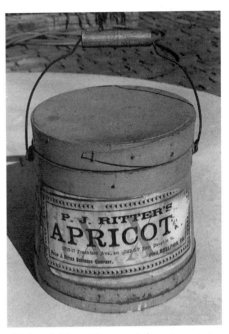

Old Judge Coffee jar with original paper label and lid. **$45**

Apricot firkin, early twentieth century, paper label. **$240**

Schoenhut lion in original condition, 1920s. **$315**

Miniature buttocks basket, double-wrapped handle, original condition. **$130**

Two late nineteenth–early twentieth century seed boxes with colorful exterior and interior labels: Philips Seeds, $335; Fisher's Seeds, $285.

Factory-made maple butter mold with impressed acorn decoration. $110

Tin spice chest, original paint and stenciled lettering. $240

Pine church bench, painted white, 9'6" long, c. 1900. $150

Oak telephones, c. 1920. **$215** each

Box of wooden printer's type, early 1900s.
$185

1950s Meadow Gold ice cream sign. **$75**

Metal Coca-Cola sign, late 1940s. **$110**

*Two bars of laundry soap in their original
wrappers.* **$8** each

Hauptmann's 10¢ cigar tin, c. 1920. **$20**

Popcorn popper, 1920s. **$50**

Six-gallon Monmouth, Illinois, stoneware crock, c. 1930. **$70**

Tin match safe, late nineteenth century. **$35**

Folger's Coffee jar, 1940s, paper label and original lid. **$15**

Refinished half-spindle-back kitchen chair, poplar, pine, and maple. **$45**

Oak spindle-back chair with pine seat, painted green. **$35**

"Firehouse" Windsor chair, painted finish with original stenciling, early 1900s. **$75**

Spindle-back kitchen chair with pine plank seat, early 1900s. **$45**

Kitchen chair with turned spindles and pine plank seat, painted red and green, c. 1920. **$40**

Brass cow bells, Collinsville, Illinois, 1930s. **$65** each

Unusual child's rocking chair, walnut with cane seat and back, c. 1890. **$145**

Papier-mâché elephant's head. **$325**

Three-drawer miniature chest, 19" tall × 12" wide, painted pine, late nineteenth century. **$155**

Papier-mâché lion's head from 1920s carnival or circus, worn as a mask. **$325**

Papier-mâché bear's head. **$325**

Child's wicker chair, early 1900s. **$45**

Cast-plaster African-American garden ornament, 1930s. **$75**

Graniteware colander, gray, c. 1920. **$40**

English grained and decorated watering can. **$95**

Wheeled-horse toy for small child to ride, original condition, 1930s–1940s. **$100**

Glass tabletop butter churn, original condition, c. 1920. **$65**

Two bars of "Japanese Crabapple" toilet soap. **$9 each**

Canvas water bag, c. 1930. **$45**

Wooden and iron wheel pattern, early 1900s. **$55**

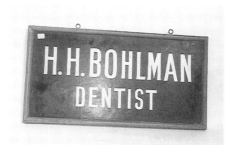

Wooden dentist's sign, 20" wide × 9" high.
$80

Copper teakettle, early 1900s. **$55**

Three brass scoops. **$20** each

Larro Feeds metal container, c. 1940. **$35**

Campbell coffee tin, Bloomington, Illinois.
$75

Fireman's helmet, original condition. **$95**

Two yellowware mixing bowls with blue stripes, 8" and 9" diameters, 1930s. **$35** *each*

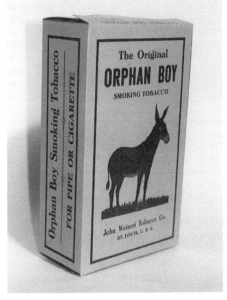

Unused box for Orphan Boy smoking tobacco. $8

Two unused boxes of Dixie Wonder Liniment. $7 each

Two unused popcorn boxes. $6 *each*

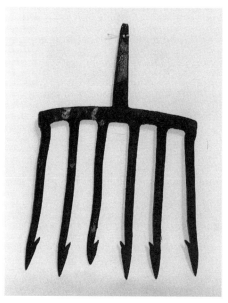

Wrought-iron frog gig. **$70**

Bait bucket with stenciled fish on the front, original condition. **$150**

Elite Tool Chest For Boys with original interior label and several tools, 1920s. **$135**

Three unused boxes of Fleetwood Tea. **$5** *each*

Individual garden seeds, unused packets. **$4** *each*

Print in original walnut frame, c. 1900. **$120**

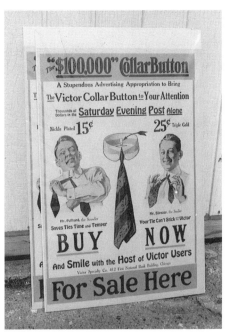

Cardboard advertisements for collar buttons, unused, 20″ × 25″. **$20** *each*

Coffee grinder, original condition, pine with cast-iron top. **$85**

Cast-iron teakettle, early 1900s. **$45**

Nickel-plated-over-copper teakettle, maple grip handle, c. 1915. **$40**

Molded cardboard owl used to frighten rodents. **$48**

Factory-made eight-drawer spice chest, early 1900s, painted. **$215**

Shoemaker's shoe last for lady's shoe, early 1900s. **$15**

Colorful holiday box, early 1900s. **$15**

Graniteware pie pan, 9½″ diameter, gray, 1920s. **$22**

Child's piano, 18″ wide × 11″ high, original condition with stenciled decoration. **$75**

Lemon or orange reamer, graniteware, gray, early 1900s. **$55**

Copake Country Auctions

Michael Fallon is an auctioneer and appraiser who conducts regularly scheduled cataloged Americana auction sales of formal and country furniture, Shaker items, quilts, coverlets, hooked rugs, samplers, and folk art. Each year the Copake Country Auction also conducts the "best bicycle sale in the world" featuring antique bicycles and related memorabilia.

Mr. Fallon is a member of the National Association of Certified Auctioneers, National Auctioneers' Association, New England Appraisers' Association, and the International Society of Appraisers.

The items that follow have been sold recently at Copake Country Auctions. Mr. Fallon may be contacted at:

Copake Country Auctions
Box H
Copake, NY 12516
Telephone: (518) 329-1142

Tin horse. **$137**

Cast-iron blinking-eye clock. **$710**

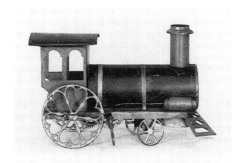

Ive's locomotive. **$550**

165

Child's buggy. **$385**

Left: *Chippendale chest,* **$1100.** Right: *Sheraton work table,* **$440.**

Hudson Valley kas. **$4125**

Peter Lorenz coverlet. **$510**

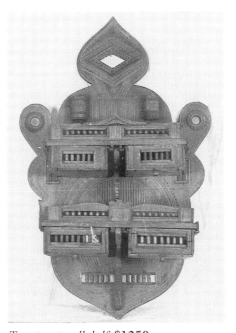

Wicker chair. **$675**

Tramp art wall shelf. **$1250**

Long Island, New York, blanket box. **$825**

Indian weather vane. **$247**

Beer tray. **$180**

Early twentieth-century hooked rug. **$500**

Early Spring Farm Antiques

(This section was prepared by Allen Hanson.)

Early Spring Farm Antiques carried its name from my business of 18 years in New York State. About 11 years ago we moved to Martha's Vineyard (an island off the coast of Cape Cod in Massachusetts) and decided to remain year round. We purchased a farmhouse on the water and brought to it the business name.

A small barn and cottage behind the house hold an inventory of eighteenth- and nineteenth-century American country furniture, folk art, quilts, nautical, and, more recently, architectural fragments, and garden items.

Most of our inventory is from the island and Cape Cod homes, which means "fresh to the market." We look for the unusual and sometimes amusing and love the search.

As I exhibit at about 18 shows a year, my teacher-husband Linc helps me. My barn is open year round. In addition, some of my furniture is used for display at the Martha's Vineyard Women's Co-op in Tisbury Market Place. It is an island-made contemporary crafts shop.

We are a stone's throw from the ferry coming into Vineyard Haven and are happy to meet boats when we can.

Early Spring Farm
93 Lagoon Pond Road
Vineyard Haven, MA 02568-9701
(508) 693-9141

Unusual squirrel cage, wood house with tin door. $125–$250

Nineteenth-century wall cupboard with drawers inside ($200–$275) sits atop a New Hampshire splayed-leg table with paint remnants, c. 1840 ($300–$400); two painted, nineteenth-century Massachusetts spindle-back chairs, $200–$300 the pair.

Primitive plant stand, green paint, $100–$190. Next to the stand sits a stoneware crock with blue bands, $50–$75. On the bottom shelf is a large redware pitcher (left) *from the late nineteenth century ($55–$75) and a large redware jug* (right) *from the early twentieth century, $48–$65.*

Cape Cod server, tiger maple, original pulls, c. 1840. $700–$1000

Garth's Auctions

Garth's Auctions, Inc. of Delaware, Ohio, is one of the nation's best-known auction sources for Americana. Garth's offers detailed and heavily illustrated catalogs by mail for each of their sales and encourages telephone bidding. Garth's makes available its catalogs and post-sale price lists by annual subscription.

All of the pieces of furniture and the textiles shown in this section were sold at recent Garth's auctions. Garth's does add a 10% buyer's premium to the gavel price of each item.

Information or a catalog subscription can be secured by contacting:

Garth's Auctions, Inc.
2690 Stratford Road, Box 369
Delaware, OH 43015
Telephone: (614) 362-4771
Fax: (614) 363-0164

Furniture

Grain-painted rope bed, poplar cleaned down to the original red-and-black graining, original round rope side rails, 48" high, $605. Pieced quilt, drunkards path in blue calico and white, embroidered black initials "U.S.T.," $330.

Country one-piece open pewter cupboard, popular with old light green repaint on all surfaces, 46" wide. $5720

Country pie safe, yellow pine with old worn and flaking finish, 12 punched tin panels with Masonic designs, found in LaGrange, Georgia. **$990**

Country one-piece pewter cupboard, walnut with old worn finish, southern Indiana or northern Kentucky. **$522**

Country side chair, refinished maple, old worn rush seat, **$275.** *Country stand, curly maple with good old dark finish, turned legs, mortised apron and one-board top,* **$715.**

Country double-wide cupboard, pine and poplar with old mellow refinishing, 106½" wide. **$4290**

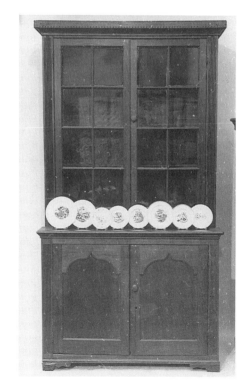

Country one-piece wall cupboard, cherry with old dark refinishing, 46" wide, eight panes of glass, molded cornice. **$1595**

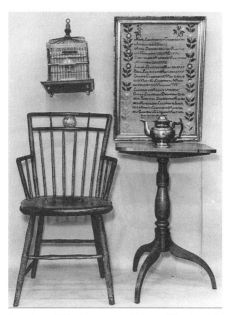

Bamboo Windsor armchair, old pinkish-putty-colored repaint with yellow striping and rose-painted back over original green, 34¾" high, $770. Country Hepplewhite candlestand, refinished curly maple with simple foliage inlay in center of top, tripod base with spider legs, $440.

Country Hepplewhite one-piece corner cupboard, refinished walnut with maple and cherry inlay, feet and hardware replaced, interior has old pale green paint, 52½" wide × 92½" high. $6380

Hoop-back bamboo Windsor side chair, highly refinished, good style with delicate turnings, seven-spindle back and molded crest rail, 37½" high, $2145 set of seven. Pewter teapot, "R. Gleason" touchmark, 8⅝" high, $275.

Pair of decorated Pennsylvania side chairs, worn original red-and-black graining with blue-and-yellow striping and polychrome floral decoration on slat and crest, 17″ seat × 33″ high, $187. Decorated washstand, pine with old worn yellow repaint with black striping, turned feet and posts, one dovetailed drawer, top with cutout for bowl and dovetailed gallery, one end of the crest is damaged and top has age cracks, $220.

Country Hepplewhite stand, walnut with worn and weathered surface with traces of old red, square tapered legs and one dovetailed drawer, drawer replaced and one-board top has age cracks, found in Virginia, **$192.** Country Chippendale side chair, maple and other hardwood with good old dark finish, minor old repairs, 16½″ seat × 37½″ high, **$418.**

Bow-back Windsor side chair, old dark varnish stain, splayed legs and H stretcher with bamboo turnings, saddle seat and nine-spindle back, underside of seat is branded "F. Trumble," 19½″ seat × 33″ high. **$550**

Primitive high chair, old red repaint, three slats, turned finials and splint seat, 39″ high, **$605.** Country mule chest, refinished pine, two dovetailed drawers, two false drawers and molded-edge top, pine and poplar secondary wood, replaced back foot, 44″ wide × 41¼″ high, **$429.** Dome-top hide-covered trunk with leather trim and brass studs, lined with early wallpaper, wrought-iron lock and end handles, wear and damage, 18½″ long, **$93.**

Country Chippendale tilt-top candlestand, mahogany with old finish, tripod base with snake feet, turned column and dish-turned one-board top, hinge block replaced and top is probably an old mismatch, 21" diameter × 27" high, **$220.** Fanback Windsor side chair, refinished, splayed base with bulbous turned legs and H stretcher, 18" seat × 35½" high, **$385.**

Country two-piece wall cupboard of walnut with old mellow refinishing, raised panel doors, three dovetailed drawers, poplar secondary wood, replaced brasses, 42" wide × 83¼" high. **$1650**

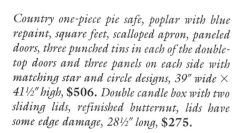

Country one-piece pie safe, poplar with blue repaint, square feet, scalloped apron, paneled doors, three punched tins in each of the double-top doors and three panels on each side with matching star and circle designs, 39" wide × 41½" high, **$506.** Double candle box with two sliding lids, refinished butternut, lids have some edge damage, 28½" long, **$275.**

Grain-painted Pennsylvania blanket chest, poplar with original red comb graining over a yellow ground, dovetailed case and dovetailed bracket feet, 47½″ wide, **$275.** *Country stool, worn black finish over old red, worn splint seat, 27½″ high,* **$148.**

Bamboo Windsor armchair, old worn black repaint, splayed legs with H stretcher, nine-spindle back, one back leg and side rung replaced, mahogany arms were not originally painted, 16½″ seat × 35″ high, **$357.** *Country Hepplewhite candlestand, refinished cherry and birch, top is warped, tripod base with spider legs with shoelike feet, turned column and square top, 28″ high,* **$220.**

Country Sheraton chest, refinished cherry, paneled ends, turned feet and corner posts with two flutes, four dovetailed drawers, 41" high × 37½" wide, $605. Shaker footstool, worn dark original finish with original label on underside of top, $522.

Country Hepplewhite work table, pine and poplar with old mellow refinishing, two overlapping dovetailed drawers, 25½" high × 50½" wide, $495. Painted dome-top box, pine with original red paint with black stripe graining, wrought-iron lock and hasp, 30" long, $77.

Country Sheraton dressing table, hard and soft woods with original graining in imitation of curly maple, paint has touch-up repair, $440. Decorated box, pine with worn original yellow paint with black striping, dovetailed, 17½" long, $192. Painted bamboo Windsor chair, old worn green repaint over black, splayed legs with H stretcher, shaped seat, spindle back and post with rabbit-ear finials, 17" seat × 33½" high, $220.

Decorated fancy Sheraton armchair, worn old black paint over red with yellow-and-gold striping and stenciled crest, 16¼″ seat × 34″ high, **$412.** Country Sheraton stand, refinished cherry and curly maple, turned legs, two dovetailed drawers and one-board top, replaced glass pulls, poplar secondary wood, **$770.**

Empire work table, refinished cherry with figured mahogany and maple veneer facade, turned legs, three dovetailed drawers, **$742.** Sheraton-style armchair, maple with old worn finish and worn rush seat, not period, 34½″ high, **$27.**

Illinois two-piece country wall cupboard, walnut with old mellow refinishing, 94¾″ tall. **$2420**

Country dry sink, refinished pine has traces of old blue, 44" wide, $440. Shaker #6 rocker, worn original dark brown finish with Mt. Lebanon label, 41½" high, $880.

Shaker armchair rocker, worn original finish, Mt. Lebanon, New York, label, 38" high, $825. Country stand, pine and poplar with old mellow refinishing, slender turned legs, one dovetailed drawer and replaced top, 30½" high, $247.

Chest made from a highboy top, maple and pine with old mellow refinishing, added turned feet, base molding and turned pulls, six dovetailed overlapping drawers and molded cornice, 36" wide. $660

Country Empire blanket chest, curly maple with old refinishing with good color and shiny over-varnish, one-board sides and ends have minor age cracks, 48½" wide. $715

Country Chippendale blanket chest, refinished poplar, bracket feet, dovetailed case, two dovetailed drawers and till, worn finish and old replaced lock in till, 49½" long. $467

Country one-piece corner cupboard, ash and other hardwoods with worn old brown graining, simple cutout feet, raised paneled doors, two nailed drawers, high pie shelf with setback shelf and molded cornice, 52" wide × 84" high. $1100

Zoar, Ohio, small cupboard, walnut with old mellow finish, poplar secondary wood, 35" high, **$1870**. Ladder-back armchair, refinished hardwood, sausage turnings, splint seat is damaged, top slat is incomplete, 45½" high, **$110**.

Cannonball rope bed, refinished pine and poplar with traces of old red finish, replaced rails, **$275**. Pieced and appliquéd quilt, stars and tulips in red and yellow calico on a white ground, 68" × 86", **$93**.

Country rope bed, old red paint, turned posts and acorn finials, original rails, **$275**. Dovetailed dough box with lid and turned handles, poplar with old red, found in Lancaster County, Pennsylvania, 32" long, **$275**.

Country two-piece open pewter cupboard with architectural detail, poplar with old dark finish, turned bun feet, feet replaced, top has been cut down and one shelf and doors removed, 43" wide × 72" high. **$1430**

Country one-piece corner cupboard, pine and poplar with old mellow refinishing, front feet replaced, interior has light blue repaint, 45" wide × 71" high. **$2860**

Pedestal from Fairhaven, Vermont, meetinghouse, pine with old alligatored reddish varnish finish, good paneled detail, wire-nail construction 16" × 16" × 33" high, **$1320** *the pair. Country jelly cupboard, pine and poplar with old dark reddish brown finish, 42" wide × 54" high plus gallery,* **$825.**

Sewer pipe boundary marker made for and used on a lot in East Liverpool, Ohio, base has molded inscription "N.U.W. 33," chips, 45" high, **$550** the pair. Country Hepplewhite chest of drawers, refinished cherry, poplar secondary wood, front feet and apron replaced, 39" wide × 44½" high, **$440.**

Comb-back armchair rocker with arrow spindles, old worn and yellowed white repaint with black and green striping and stenciled grapes, arms have old natural finish, **$550.** Country Sheraton washstand, refinished pine, turned legs and posts with base shelf and dovetailed gallery, **$412.**

Country two-piece wall cupboard, cherry with old mellow refinishing, hardware replaced and some pieced repairs, 52″ wide × 83½″ high. **$4345**

Hepplewhite two-piece corner cupboard, cherry with old mellow refinishing, poplar secondary wood, original brass knobs, 48½″ wide × 88¼″ high. **$6325**

Paint-decorated blanket chest, pine with original red flame graining, turned feet, dovetailed case with applied base and lid molding, till with lid, 38″ wide, **$550**. Decorated highback armchair rocker, worn original green paint with black and gold striping and stenciled fruit, flowers and foliage decoration, 41″ high, **$550**.

Country Empire chest of drawers, curly maple with good figure throughout and old refinishing, turned walnut pulls are replaced, poplar secondary wood, 43″ high. **$990**

Decorated plank-seat side chair, very worn original red flame graining on a salmon pink ground, black striping, 32¾″ high, **$693** set of 6. Small cupboard, poplar with old dark reddish brown finish, 29¾″ high, **$880**. Hanging candle box, walnut with original finish, dovetailed case, one dovetailed drawer, lift top and shaped crest, drawer bottom is an old replacement, **$660**.

Country jelly cupboard, pine with old worn red repaint, raised panel doors set in beaded frames and molded cornice, 37½″ wide × 64″ high. **$2530**

Country mule chest, hardwood and pine with blue repaint, drawers have never had pulls, one foot is incomplete, 44″ wide × 45¼″ high. **$440**

Country cupboard, pine cleaned down to old bluish green, 44″ wide × 70″. **$990**

Country one-piece wall cupboard, pine with worn blue repaint over salmon, paneled doors, high pie shelf with scalloped rail, 44¼″ wide × 79″ high. **$1980**

Hanging shelf, walnut with old finish but speckles of white paint, twentieth century, 13″ wide × 32″ high, **$192.** *Ladder-back wagon seat, refinished and replaced splint seat, 33¾″ long,* **$187.** *Country one-piece step-back wall cupboard, poplar with worn old yellow combed repaint, single-board doors, 71½″ high,* **$990.**

Ohio decorated two-piece wall cupboard, pine with original red sponge graining on case and graining in imitation of curly maple on the doors and drawers, original hardware, 90¼″ high × 47½″ wide. **$3080**

Country one-piece corner cupboard, poplar with old worn cream-colored repaint, 47″ wide × 85″ high, **$3465.** *Cast-iron eagle, old worn and weathered black, white and yellow paint, 33½″ high,* **$2090.**

Continuous-arm Windsor chair, splayed base with bulbous turnings and H stretcher, 18″ seat × 36¾″ high. **$7150**

Architectural two-piece corner cupboard, pine with old cream and salmon repaint, butterfly shelves, 60" wide × 101" high. **$2970**

Bamboo Windsor side chairs, old black repaint with gold striping, 35" high, **$2805** set of six. Country work table, hardwood with old worn and alligatored black paint with red striping and white trim, pieced repair to applied-edge gallery, 27½" high, **$440**.

Fanback Windsor side chair, old refinishing has a nut brown color, splayed base with bulbous turnings and H stretcher, old repairs and replacements and one front leg is a nonmatching replacement, 34¾" high. **$412.50**

Miniature cupboard made from the base of a grandfather's clock, cherry with old worn finish, pine top added, 26" high, **$275**. Shaker ladder-back armchair rocker, hardwood with old dark finish, 41¾" high, **$715**.

Semicircular three-tier crock stand, soft wood cleaned down to old red, 58″ wide × 28″ deep × 32½″ high. **$275**

Country Windsor high chair, legs and one arm are old replacements, 38″ high, $192. Country cradle, pine with old worn dark red finish, mortised and pinned construction with cutout headboard and slats, 39″ long, $375.

Water bench, pine with old red paint, shoe feet, double doors in base, beaded-edge stiles and end boards with scalloped top edges, 32" wide × 64" high. **$1705**

Textiles

Pieced quilt, Ohio stars in solid red and medium blue, white calico and red and blue border, 76" × 79". **$440**

Pieced quilt, pineapple log cabin in two shades of brown calico and solid medium blue, 77" × 95". **$660**

Appliqué quilt, nine oak-leaf pinwheels with star centers in olive green and red with grid, 78½" × 81". **$165**

Pieced quilt, black prints with white diagonal slashes in a pink and maroon print grid, Pennsylvania origin, 79" × 82". **$715**

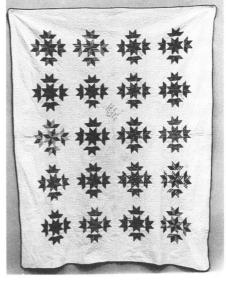

Pieced quilt, 16 pinwheel squares in solid goldenrod and green calico, Indiana origin, minor damage, 75" × 76". **$495**

Pieced album or friendship quilt, 20 star medallions in pink and brown prints and solid blue and green, "Presented to T.J. Halsted by the Shilo Class, July the 13, 1876," 69" × 84". **$605**

Appliqué quilt, floral center surrounded by eight treelike designs, stylized flowers and meandering border with round "buds" in solid red and green with yellow calico, 90" × 91".
$935

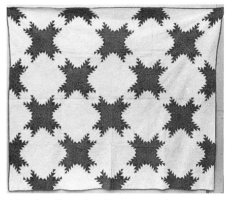

Pieced quilt, red calico stars with green sawtooth edges, stains with some tears and several repaired slashes along one edge, 81" × 96".
$550

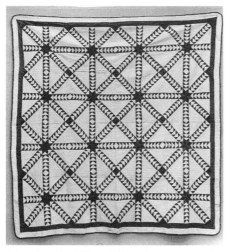

Pieced quilt, 87" × 89", grid in green calico and white with red and green star centers.
$440

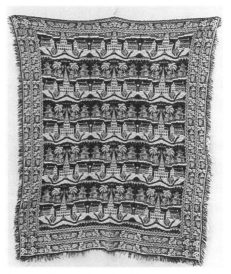

Jacquard one-piece double-weave coverlet, Boston town design and vintage borders, navy blue and natural white, minor wear and moth damage and minor stains, 62" × 74".
$385

Left: *Jacquard coverlet, labeled "Made by Samuel Dornback, Sugarloaf, Luzerne Co for ————Penn. 1845,"* 85" × 88", **$302.** Center: *Jacquard one-piece single-weave coverlet, floral medallions, labeled "Made by J. Hausman in Lobachsville, 1846," red, olive green, deep yellow and natural white,* 78" × 101", **$495.** Right: *Jacquard coverlet, labeled "Made by Samuel Dornbach, Sugarloaf, Luzerne Co for————Penn. 1845," red, navy blue and medium green, stains and a little fringe loss,* 82" × 89", **$440.**

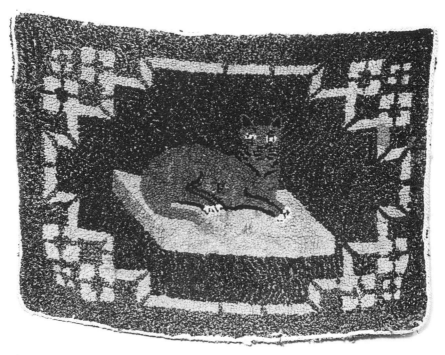

Hooked-yarn rag rug, loosely hooked and some fading, repair and damage but very folksy, 25½" × 35½". **$225**

Top row. Left: Ohio sampler, silk on linen homespun, "Wrought by Sally Jane Austin, Mansfield, August 1834," 18½" high × 19¼" wide, $3630. Right: Sampler, silk on linen homespun, "C.E.G. Anno 1774," 19¼" high × 16¼" wide, $770. Bottom row. Left: Sampler, silk on finely woven linen homespun, "Besheba Reynolds, the Happy Choice ... 1806," 17¾" high × 14¼" wide, $385. Right: Sampler, silk on linen homespun, "Susannah Garrick her work in the eleventh year of her age 1797," wear damage and stains, 16" high × 14" wide, $55.

Appliqué quilt, six stylized baskets with flowers and puffed berries in green, red, and goldenrod with pink calico, 75" × 100". $880

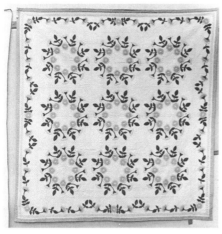

Appliqué quilt, roses and buds in two shades of pink, pale yellow and grayish teal green, minor stains, 85″ × 86″. **$990**

Appliqué quilt, nine stylized floral medallions in red, green, and yellow calico, four feather-quilted wreaths, wear, stains, and fading, one corner marked "Joseph F. Ford," 84″ × 88″. **$440**

Appliqué quilt, 12 roses each surrounded by buds in red and green with pink calico, red and yellow embroidered detail on the buds is incomplete, small holes, wear and stains, binding is machine sewn, 72″ × 89″. **$247**

Amish pieced quilt, black and mint green sateen, well quilted, 75″ × 80″. **$770**

198

Pieced quilt, Lancaster County, Pennsylvania, calico with deep rust red and gray in sawtooth design, small stains, 87″ × 87″. **$957**

Appliqué quilt, nine stylized floral medallions in deep red and black calico, well quilted with four petal and feather medallions between the appliqués, binding is machine sewn, wear and stains, 79″ × 80″. **$412**

Appliqué quilt, summer weight with no batting, quilting follows the edge of the appliqué, minor wear, overall stain with a few dark spots, binding is machine sewn, 83″ × 97″. **$715**

Left: *Jacquard two-piece single-weave coverlet, "H. Petry, Canton, Stark County, Ohio, 1839," worn, repairs, and fringe incomplete, 63" × 80",* **$275.** Center: *Jacquard two-piece double-weave coverlet, navy blue, natural white, and salmon, eagle medallions, very worn with damage, 74" × 90",* **$302.** Right: *Jacquard one-piece single-weave coverlet, central floral medallion with floral borders and angels in the corners, worn, some damage, and fringe loss, 72" × 76",* **$137.**

Left: *Sampler, silk on homespun linen, "Hannah Albertson 1813," some fading and stains, 28½" high × 23" wide,* **$770.** Right, top: *Needlework memorial on silk, pen-and-ink inscription on tomb, lovely old colors in shades of blue, green, pink, brown, gold, and white, silk is badly stained and has small holes, 18¼" high × 19¼" wide,* **$330.** Right, bottom: *Needlework panel, wool satin stitch on holy family in shades of brown, olive, and white with gray, blue, and red, wear and old rebacking on burlap, 18" high × 20½" wide,* **$110.**

Top row. Left: *Sampler, silk on linen homespun, "Amanda Brody, Aimwell School, 1st Month 1829, Philadelphia," 20" high × 20¾" wide,* **$935.** Right: *Sampler, silk on homespun, "Mary Jane Campbell, Born June 28, 1811, Steubenville, Ohio, 1820," 18¾" high × 13¾" wide,* **$990.** *Bottom row.* Left: *Sampler, silk on homespun, "Jane Myers 1827," some fading but colors are still good, stains and some wear, 13½" high × 13" wide,* **$990.** Right: *Sampler, wool and silk on homespun, "Death of a Sister . . . July 6, 1836," 13½" high × 13" wide,* **$660.**

Lancaster Antique Market

The *New York Times* has called the Lancaster Antique Market "the best small-town antiques center in Kentucky." The 10,000 square-foot market specializes in Americana and country antiques. Owner Ellen Tatem produces a monthly videotape of recent acquisitions. The 30–40 minute narrated video may be purchased by mail for $10. Antiques are shipped daily by United Parcel Service and freight to customers across the United States.

Additional information may be secured by contacting:

Lancaster Antique Market
102 Hamilton Avenue
P.O. Box 553
Lancaster, KY 40444
Telephone: (606) 792-4536

Rooster ornament from a fence post. **$395**

Wall box for candles, red paint, square nails. **$125**

Early one-drawer stand with turned legs and original painted finish. **$345**

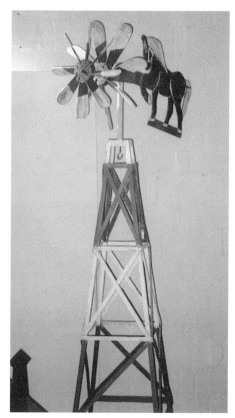

Tall wooden windmill with ornamental horse. **$195**

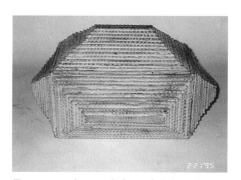

Tramp art box with hinged lid, pale blue paint. **$295**

Box of children's china dishes in original container. **$175**

Early cupboard with H hinges and panel door in original mustard paint, wooden pegs on the inside for hanging garments. **$950**

Collection of country items including a table in blue paint with turned legs and a single drawer. **$795**

Child's twig chair, brown paint. **$145**

Gate with traces of mustard paint. **$145**

Early butter scales ($295) and mortised window ($195).

Large watercolor of fish, ornamental frame. $575

Plant stand, pine, green paint. $350

Boxes covered in early paper. Bottom: **$195.**
Middle: **$65**

Pie safe, blue paint, star tins. **$750**

New Hampshire blanket chest, gray paint. **$1450**

Early pine-top table with drawer and tapered legs. **$695**

Early bucket bench, H hinges on doors and dovetailed drawers at the top. **$2500**

Step-back blind-front cupboard, original mustard paint. **$2950**

Primitive Kentucky sugar chest with drawer and hoof feet, red paint. **$1750**

Shaker bucket, chrome yellow paint. **$495**

Market basket, green paint. **$245**

Child's step-back cupboard with glass doors, gray and mustard paint. **$495**

One-drawer walnut stand. **$195**

Youth chair with traces of red paint. **$95**

Early chair in bittersweet and black paint, Kentucky origin. **$345**

Quail Country Antiques

Quail Country Antiques is a 13-member collective located in Walnut Creek, California, 35 minutes east of San Francisco. An extensive selection of American country antiques is displayed in a charming 90-year-old California cottage. The emphasis at Quail Country is on painted furniture, stoneware, textiles, folk art, toys, and garden-related antiques.

The shop is open during the months of November and December from 10 A.M. to 5 P.M., Monday through Saturday and 11 A.M. to 4 P.M. on Sunday. Shipping is available.

Quail Country Antiques
1581 Boulevard Way
Walnut Creek, CA 94595
(510) 944-0930

Stitchery sampler. **$295**

Country pie safe, cream paint. **$1200**

Cherry two-drawer table, red wash. **$995**

Dry sink, light blue paint, Kentucky. **$1400**

One-drawer stand, mustard paint. **$385**

Dough box, dark blue paint, Pennsylvania.
$650

Jelly cupboard, red paint, Connecticut.
$1800

Windsor rocking chair. **$695**

Pair of blue ladder-back fireside chairs, blue paint, **$145** *each. One-drawer pine stand, red wash,* **$395.**

Kentucky pie safe, dark blue paint. **$2495**

"Welcome" hooked rug. **$295**

Cabin in the snow hooked rug, New England. **$495**

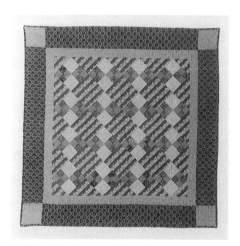

Crib quilt, four-patch variation on point, late 19th century. **$395**

Sunflower quilt, dark green and pumpkin calico, New York, c. 1880. **$995**

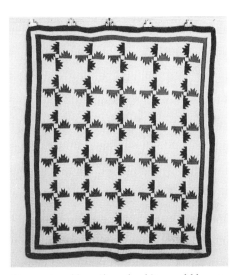

Amish double Irish-chain quilt, lavender and black, Lancaster County, Pennsylvania, c. 1920. **$1195**

Kansas trouble quilt, red, white, and blue, attributed to Martha Wampler of Bicknel, Indiana, c. 1890. **$1150**

Ross cat-pattern hooked rug, canvas. **$225**

Sampler, dated 1825. **$895**

New Jersey sampler, Hannah Peterson, 1832–1870. **$550**

Silk sampler, 1848. **$895**

Primitive game board, cream, black, and red. **$395**

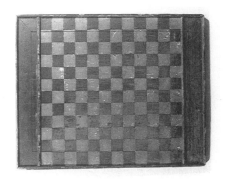

Red and mustard game board. **$495**

Stamped bucket, blue and white. **$325**

Bandboxes: Top, **$195**; bottom, **$265.**

Stack of painted firkins: Gray, **$195**; *red,* **$295**; *blue,* **$325**; *green,* **$475.**

214

Bookplate, Pennsylvania, 1847. **$395**

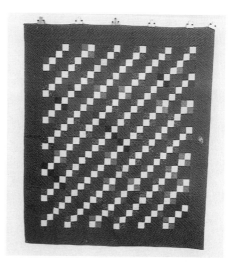

Blue-and-white quilt, four-patch. **$595**

Tinnie. **$245**

Large candle box, blue-green paint. **$485**

Brightly painted folk art wind house. **$195**

Child's Adirondack chair, red paint. **$160**

Potato-stamp decorated basket. **$165**

Pennsylvania redware, left to right: **$285, $285, $155.**

Burger salt-glaze crock. **$345**

Shutter with candlestick cutout, green paint.
$75

Wood and matchstick folk art box, heart motif. **$175**

Miniature Shaker bonnet. **$195**

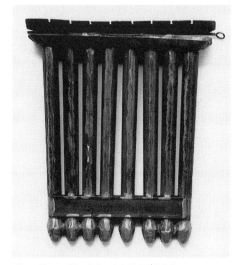

Small candle-mold holder, black paint. **$350**

Candle mold with wick lid. **$185**

Candle mold, pink, blue, and white paint.
$195

Doll chair, blue paint, $125; Amish doll,
$165; Amish Kavli, $195.

Cutlery box, blue paint. $165

Spice box, mustard paint. $295

Stick sponge and spatterware: Creamer, $129; plate, $165; handleless cup, $225.

Blue sponge cooler, unglazed. $295

Milk stool, red wash seat. $68

Chocolate molds: Duck, $68; double lovebirds, $175; pig, $125.

3rd Sunday Market

The 3rd Sunday Market is held at the McLean County Fairgrounds in Bloomington, Illinois, from May through October. More than 400 antiques and collectibles dealers from throughout the Midwest participate each month.

The items that follow were offered for sale at the 3rd Sunday Market during the 1994 season. The value shown is the actual sticker price of the item.

Northern Seeds counter display box, colorful interior and exterior labels. **$300**

3rd Sunday Market
P.O. Box 396
Bloomington, IL 61702-0396
(309) 452-7926

Cast-iron eagle from Oklahoma gas station, c. 1930, 33½″ tall. **$1500**

Metal Ex-Lax thermometer, original condition, 1940s. **$95**

White Castle "King Size" coffee mug, 1950s. **$45**

Blown glass jar, original tin lid, 23" tall, late nineteenth century. **$475**

Dr. Hobson's Oriental Hair Restorer bottle, original paper label. **$35**

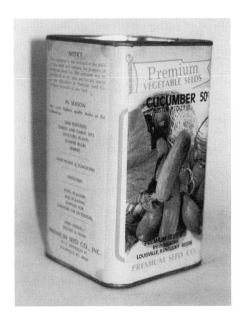

Vegetable seed container with pouring spout, c. 1950. **$15**

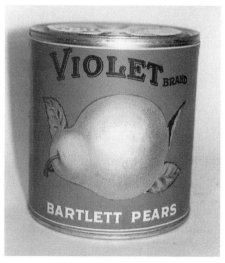

Unused can of Violet Bartlett Pears, paper label, c. 1950. **$9**

Unused can of Minton's Choice Bartlett Pears, c. 1950. **$9**

Unused can of Burnham Bartlett Pears, c. 1950. **$9**

Premium Seeds container with pouring spout, c. 1950. **$25**

Powdered Opium can, early 1900s, paper label. **$95**

Eel-River Valley Lodge lantern, early 1900s. **$335**

Button's Raven Gloss Shoe Dressing box, pine, paper label. **$150**

Gold-Prize Coffee clock, pine case, early 1900s. **$800**

Storage container for "Bill Heads," English, late nineteenth century. $65

Nineteenth-century Somerset Garden Seeds box, original paper labels. $245

Grand Union Tea Company coffee mill, original painted surface, c. 1910. $450

Blown glass storage jar, late nineteenth century. $85

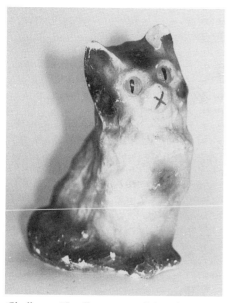

Chalk cat, 7" tall, worn condition. **$22**

Feather Christmas tree, cobalt blue, turned base, 14" tall, c. 1920. **$335**

Santa Claus, filled with straw, original condition, 26" tall, c. 1930. **$345**

Santa Claus, filled with straw, original condition, 28½" tall, 1930s. **$400**

Elephant stuffed toy, 36" tall, 1940s. **$125**

Halloween parade torch for candle, c. 1920, 8" diameter. **$300**

Jack-o'-lantern with skeleton face, wire hanger, 1940s. **$165**

Molded paper jack-o'-lantern, wire handle, 1940s. **$95**

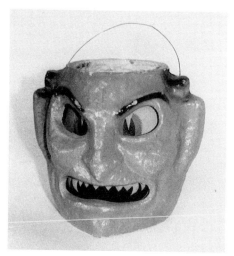

"Devil" jack-o'-lantern made of molded paper, original painted liner, wire hanger, 1940s. **$150**

"Smiling" jack-o'-lantern with original paper liner, 1940s–1950s. **$85**

Miniature jack-o'-lantern made of molded paper, c. 1950, 5" diameter. **$65**

Halloween "cat" lantern made of pressed and molded paper, original paper liner, 1940–1950. **$110**

Unusual jack-o'-lantern with ears, original paper liner, 1940s. **$260**

229

Pair of child's suede boots, 1940s. **$45**

Birdhouse, 1940s, original condition. **$57**

Noah's ark, original condition, early 1900s, original animals and Noah, damage to deck area. **$875**

Glass flask with pewter top, c. 1920. **$50**

Carved wood sheep with wool covering, bell at neck, early 1900s, 4″ long. **$55**

Shaker-type woven gathering basket, 33" diameter, New England. **$440**

Storage basket, oak splint, Native-American origin, painted blue, 8½" long × 4½" deep. **$210**

Storage basket, oak splint, "kicked in" bottom, 10" diameter. **$145**

Pennsylvania-rye straw basket. **$65**

Storage or utility basket, oak splint, carved handle, 10½" diameter. **$85**

Half basket, carved handle, rib construction, oak splint. **$145**

Painted knife-and-fork box, carved handle, early twentieth century, oak splint. **$250**

Herb drying basket, Shaker-type, New England origin, 11" diameter. **$330**

Painted storage basket with lid, 7½" diameter at top. **$185**

Native-American storage basket, 8" long × 4½" wide. **$55**

Cast-iron rabbit, 9″ tall, worn original surface. **$200**

Cast-iron rabbit, original painted surface, used as a doorstop, c. 1930. **$235**

Twenty-gallon Red Wing, Minnesota, crock. **$57**

Ten-gallon water cooler, midwestern origin, slip-trailed decoration. **$235**

Stoneware storage crock with Rockingham glaze, early twentieth century, no maker's mark. $75

Shaker berry pail, painted red, iron bands, drop handle with maple grip, New England, early twentieth century. $315

American eagle butter print, machine-impressed decoration. $260

Butter print with impressed wheat decoration, 3½" diameter, original finish. $90

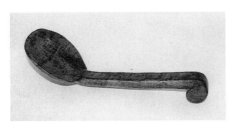

Butter worker made from tiger maple, nineteenth century. $145

Galvanized tin scoop, 8" long. $15

Heart-decorated butter print, lathe turned with hand-carved decoration, late nineteenth century, 4½″ diameter. **$325**

Turned maple pestle. **$22**

Green-painted Shaker fingered oval box, New England, maple sides with pine top and bottom, copper nails, 12″ long. **$750**

Shaker box, original unpainted finish, 12″ long, maple and pine, copper nails, New England. **$425**

Walnut scrubbing board, factory-made, late nineteenth century. **$125**

Staved buckets, wooden bands, painted finish, drop handles: Small sugar bucket, **$150**; *large bucket, 9" diameter,* **$175.**

Sugar bucket with button-hole hoops, painted red, 10" diameter. **$245**

Tin spice chest with original stenciled decoration and lettering. **$585**

Bucket, blue paint, staved construction, overlapping bands. **$200**

Lathe-turned funnel, maple. **$95**

Two-tube candle mold, tin, rare form. **$165**

Maple scoop made from a single piece of wood, 15½″ long, used in a grocery store for flour or sugar. **$215**

Rolling or noodle board, 22″ diameter, painted green, possibly European in origin. **$165**

Carved tasting spoon, made from a single piece of walnut, nineteenth century, possibly European in origin. **$55**

237

Chopping knife, early twentieth century. **$45**

One snow shoe, original condition, c. 1930. **$45**

Enterprise #2 coffee mill, cast iron, original stenciling and drawer. **$475**

Buggy wheel, original condition, painted green. **$54**

Pine dry sink, painted blue, child's size, 34″ wide × 22″ deep × 30″ high, early twentieth century. **$485**

Copper wash boiler with original lid and handles, c. 1930. **$60**

Firehouse Windsor chairs, early twentieth century, refinished. **$325** *set of four*

Pair of hooked gloves, early twentieth century, colorful. **$150**

Pair of hooked mittens, early twentieth century, colorful, New England. **$225**

CHAPTER TEN

Country Store Antiques

Notes for Collectors

- One of the joys and advantages of collecting country store antiques is that significant examples can be found literally almost anywhere because of the proliferation of rural and neighborhood grocery stores during the 1880–1940 period.

- The 1880–1940 era is considered by collectors the "golden age" of the American grocery store because that time frame predated the supermarket. The emerging supermarket forever altered the way that companies packaged, advertised, marketed, and displayed their products.

- Locally produced and packaged products tend to have significantly more value in the immediate area of their manufacture than in the rest of the United States. A coffee tin from a Bloomington, Illinois, maker is worth several times its Burlington, Vermont, value in Bloomington, Illinois, because of the interest of local collectors.

- There are also numerous store-related products that have established national values rather than locally influenced values. Pepsi-Cola, Coca-Cola, and Sleepy Eye products are some of the store-related items seriously collected by individuals throughout the United States.

- Condition is a paramount factor in determining value. If a cigar box has had its paper label restored or has been repaired with glued-together pieces, its worth has been dramatically compromised. Unlike a piece of country furniture that can be repaired and still maintain much of its value, the vast majority of country store memorabilia cannot.

- There are a growing number of speciality shows each year that feature advertising and country store antiques.

Key Dates in the Evolution of the Country Store

1890—Chewing tobacco is the most popular tobacco product, and hundreds of varieties are available to consumers. Each brand offers boxes, packages, tin containers, and advertising.

1910—Cigars replace chewing tobacco in popularity, and an equally large collection of brands, boxes, and advertising materials are created.

1920—Cigarettes replace cigars among the nation's smokers and the barrage of new products rekindles.

1937—Shopping carts and supermarkets gradually begin to appear in selected urban areas.

1940s—National brands replace locally marketed products on the shelves of the newly built supermarkets.

Baker's Chocolate 1916 calendar. $150–$160

Royal Crown Cola 1936 calendar. $60–$65

"No Dancing" sign. **$18–$22**

Possum cigar box. **$200–$250**

Quaker White Oats tin. **$75–$80**

Sample container of Wild Cherry snuff. **$65–$70**

American Ace harmonica in original box. **$45–$55**

Fast Mail cigars. **$135–$145**

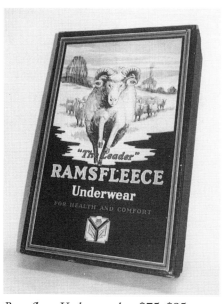

Ramsfleece Underwear box. $75–$95

Myopia Club Whiskey bottle. $60–$65

Peter Rabbit Peanut Butter container. $500–$575

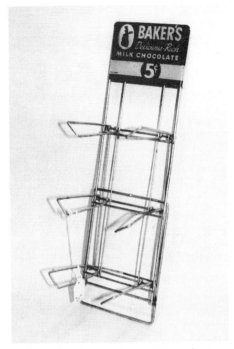

Baker's Chocolate display rack. $70–$80

Roofus the Rooster and original box, 1940s.
$25–$30

State Fair Rolled Oats cardboard container.
$100–$120

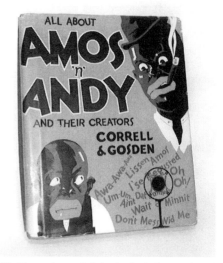

All About Amos 'n' Andy *book.* **$100–$125**

Prudential Knitted Sport Coat box.
$75–$85

Reg'lar Fellers *and* Smitty *books.* **$25–$35**
each

Huntley and Palmer biscuit tin, "May bas-
ket." **$200–$250**

C-I-L Ammunition broadside. **$250–$300**

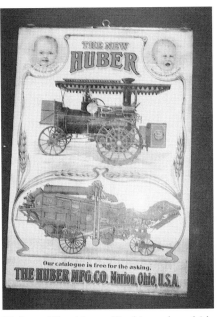

Huber Threshing Machine broadside. **$300–$400**

Sunset Trail cigars. **$375–$425**

Holstein #6 bell for sheep, Collinsville, Illinois. **$75–$115**

Orcico Cigars tin. $350–$400

Jell-o recipe book with Rose O'Neill illustrations. $70–$80

Indian Ax cigars. $110–$130

Myopia Club Whiskey bottle. $85–$100

Texie cigars. $125–$150

Toys from child's miniature country store, made from paper. **$10** *each*

Robert J. Pierce's Empress Tablets tin. **$70–$85**

Master's Choice cigar tin. **$100–$135**

Unopened boxes of Robin Hood rim-fire cartridges. **$800–$1000** *each*

Final Examination

In each of the previous 13 versions of this book we have offered a series of questions to test your ability to recall elements of the text and estimate the retail values of selected examples of Americana. Over the years individuals who have scored poorly have been threatened with a variety of potentially perverse penalties ranging from having their names written on the chalkboard to having their parents contacted directly.

We have recently had several offers of corporate sponsorship for the Final Examination preparation booklet and requests for a semi-annual international reunion of the High Achievers Club. The High Achievers Club (HAC) consists of selected individuals who scored at or above the 8th percentile on the previous Final Examination.

We have refused these inducements until this edition because we wanted to maintain the validity and reliability of the test, and we were fearful of corporate intervention and potential takeover in the process.

In an attempt to show his good faith, Mr. Elmer Almond of Yazoo Bayou, Mississippi, is offering members of the HAC a businessman's lunch at his locally revered Elmer's Eats on Stringtown Road. The lunch consists of the following:

1 can of King Oscar Sardines with tomato
1 12 oz. bottle of Dr. Pepper
2 Saltines with extra salt
1 Moon Pie
1 Goo Goo Cluster

All Mr. Almond wants in return for his generous offer is the opportunity to meet and greet High Achievers Club members who are in at least semi-good standing. We have indicated to him that we will be polling the membership about the corporate affiliation shortly.

We would suggest that you make it a point to get the businessman's special to go, leave your children in the car with the doors locked and the motor running, and do *not* ask Mr. Almond about his belt buckle or what happened to him in the sixth grade.

Directions

1. Read each question carefully.
2. Select the best response.
3. Do *not* give Mr. Almond your telephone number *or* shoe size.
4. Begin.

Matching

Match the letter on the right with the response on the left that best completes it.

_____ 1. provenance
_____ 2. overpainted
_____ 3. incised
_____ 4. stenciled
_____ 5. ovoid
_____ 6. late
_____ 7. early
_____ 8. blind front
_____ 9. breadboard ends
_____ 10. glazed
_____ 11. picker
_____ 12. pieced out
_____ 13. married
_____ 14. patina
_____ 15. smalls

a. wholesaler
b. added to
c. glass
d. a natural finish
e. baskets, buttermolds, glass jars
f. two pieces joined together but not created at the same time
g. history
h. no glass
i. technique used to decorate molded stoneware
j. pear-shaped

252

k. scratched

l. 3 or 4 coats

m. not very old

n. used to keep a tabletop from warping

o. old

Multiple Choice/True or False

16. This cupboard could best be described as

    a. glazed

    b. a step-back

    c. eighteenth century

    d. none of the above

17. This cupboard is probably made of

    a. oak

    b. hickory

    c. ash

    d. pine

18. The cupboard would be worth more with early blue paint than with early green paint.

    __ True

    __ False

19. The cupboard appears to be "married."

    __ True

    __ False

20. This cupboard in "early" yellow paint is worth more than $1,200.

    __ True

    __ False

21. The cupboard is more likely to be made of poplar than oak.

    __ True

    __ False

22. The cupboard appears to date from the 1800–1830 period.

    __ True

    __ False

23. Check the statements below that are true.

    __ The chairs date from about 1810.

    __ The chairs could best be described as spindle-backs.

    __ The seats of the chairs are probably made of pine.

__ The chairs are worth a minimum of $850.

__ These chairs could have been purchased from their maker as late as 1860.

__ These chairs are made of a combination of oak and poplar.

24. This jug dates prior to 1860.

__ True

__ False

25. The jug is probably made of redware rather than stoneware.

__ True

__ False

26. A jug of this vintage could have stenciled decoration.

__ True

__ False

27. Stoneware with an incised bird or large flower probably predates a similar example with a brushed bird or flower.

__ True

__ False

28. This mug was made in

   a. Ohio

   b. New York

   c. Illinois

   d. could have been any of the above

29. This piece was handthrown on a potter's wheel and then the decoration was attached to the mug before the glazing process.

__ True

__ False

30. This miniature Christmas tree dates from about 1830.

___ True

___ False

31. The majority of feather trees that collectors are finding today were made in

   a. America

   b. Mexico

   c. Germany

   d. England

32. A 6′ feather tree with its original stenciled box/holder would be worth

   a. about $175

   b. about $250

   c. about $400

   d. more than $550

33. Graniteware is also known as

   a. enamel

   b. agate

   c. porcelain

   d. all of the above

34. Which group of graniteware colors listed below would be considered the rarest?

   a. green, brown, copper red

   b. blue, gray, white

   c. cobalt blue, gray

   d. all are equally difficult to find

35. Older pieces of graniteware tend to be lighter in weight than more contemporary examples.

___ True

___ False

36. This gooseneck coffeepot in gray is worth more than $75.

___ True

___ False

37. This is an example of a half-spindle Boston rocking chair.

___ True

___ False

41. This rocking chair could be best described as a Windsor.

___ True

___ False

38. The chair would certainly date prior to 1820.

___ True

___ False

39. In all probability this chair is made entirely of maple.

___ True

___ False

40. Many nineteenth-century rocking chairs had seats of ____ and arms of ____.

a. oak and walnut

b. walnut and mahogany

c. pine and oak

d. pine and cherry

42. This chair dates from the late 1700s.

___ True

___ False

43. Check the statements below that are true about the cupboard.

___ It is a blind front.

___ It dates from about 1850.

___ It has batten doors.

___ It was factory-made.

44. The cupboard is worth less than $1,000.

___ True

___ False

45. The "fishing" basket could also be described as a creel.

___ True

___ False

46. The basket is worth a minimum of $45.

___ True

___ False

47. It was handcrafted rather than factory-made.

___ True

___ False

48. The box with eight individual spice containers dates no earlier than the fourth quarter of the nineteenth century.

___ True

___ False

49. The box and eight containers are worth at least $175.

___ True

___ False

50. This walnut cupboard would be a "great buy" for $3,500.

___ True

___ False

Essay (5 bonus points)

Please use the blue test booklet that was included in your packet of materials. You will get a telephone call about the red test booklet. *Please* do not break the seal.

Question: Why would Leo Gorcey be a collector of sweet shop or soda fountain memorabilia?

Answers

1. g

2. l

3. k

4. i

5. j

6. m

7. o

8. h

9. n

10. c

11. a

12. b

13. f

14. d

15. e

16. b

17. d

18. true

19. false

20. true

21. true

22. false

23. The seats of the chairs are probably made of pine.
The chairs are worth a minimum of $850.
These chairs could have been purchased from their maker as late as 1860.

24. true

25. false

26. false

27. true

28. Illinois

29. false

30. false

31. Germany

32. d

33. d

34. a

35. false

36. true

37. false

38. false

39. false

40. d

41. false

42. false

43. It is a blind front.
It has batten doors.

44. true

45. true

46. true

47. false

48. true

49. false

50. false